When Scorpio Ruled The World

Chris Stubbs

TRAFFORD
Publishing

Order this book online at www.trafford.com
or email orders@trafford.com

Most Trafford titles are also available at major online book retailers.

Note for Librarians: A cataloguing record for this book is available from Library
and Archives Canada at www.collectionscanada.ca/amicus/index-e.html

Printed in the United States of America.

ISBN: 978-1-4269-6028-4 (sc)
ISBN: 978-1-4269-6029-1 (e)

Trafford rev. 03/07/2011

 www.trafford.com

North America & international
toll-free: 1 888 232 4444 (USA & Canada)
phone: 250 383 6864 ♦ fax: 812 355 4082

I shall always be indebted to my parents,

Edward (1907-1988) and Anastasia (1909-2000) {née Bolger}

Stubbs, without whose expert guidance, wise counsel

and encouragement I should never have had the opportunity

to write this book.

Foreword

This book tries to satisfy the requirements of the first stage of two regarding the proof of the truth of Natal Astrology, i.e. the validity of Astrological Interpretation for describing a person's character. Traditionally we have relied solely on the interpretation of the person's Birth chart but this has not always proved satisfactory. Accordingly, we now introduce a new method, based on our genetic understanding of the Birth process that consists of combining the interpretation of the Epoch chart with that of the Birth chart, both of which have been cast using the Morinus House system as the "Method of Choice". To show this we produce objective and individual Person Summaries of several (in)famous conquerors from history and combine these with the appropriate biographical material to generate realistic and acceptable mini-biographies. I consider that this exercise has worked well and it has been extended to include mini-biographies for Julius Caesar and for Alexander the Great. Consequently, we should now be ready to undertake the second stage of the proof of the truth of Natal Astrology, namely the scientific investigation of "The Pre-Natal Epoch".

"If God were to hold out enclosed in His right hand all Truth,
And in His left hand just the active search for Truth,
Though with the condition that I should ever err therein,
And should say to me: Choose!
I should humbly take His left hand and say:
Father! Give me this one; absolute Truth is thine, alone."

G. E. Lessing (1729-1781), *Wolfenbüttler Fragmente*

Wirral, Merseyside, U.K.
2011
- -

CONTENTS

I should like to thank my wife, Angela, for her organisational contribution to the book and for proofreading it. My thanks must also go to Mrs J. Jackson and to Mrs J. I. Mills for proofreading the entire manuscript.

CHAPTER 1

Symbols and Basic Astrology

We can consider that the principles of the planets, as a first approximation, represent the components of consciousness, as shown in the following Table:

Personal Planets			Generation Planets		
Symbol	Name	Principle/Component	Symbol	Name	Principle/Component
☉	Sun	Will, Aim, Self-expression.	♃	Jupiter	Enthusiasm, Expansion, Generosity.
☽	Moon	Feeling, Response, Emotion	♄	Saturn	Sense of Lack , Fear, Cold, Limitation, Control.
☿	Mercury	Mentality, Communication	⚷	Chiron	Healing, Help, Philanthropy, Charity.
♀	Venus	Harmony, Affection, Relatedness	♅	Uranus	Independence, Sudden change.
♂	Mars	Initiative, Force, Energy, Desire.	♆	Neptune	Nebulousness, Fluidity, Impressionability
			♇	Pluto	Stimulation, Compulsion, Ease of Discarding, Renewal.

Retrograde describes the apparently backwards (rather than direct) motion of a planet when seen from the Earth. Stationary describes a planet's situation when it changes from direct to retrograde motion or vice-versa. When a planet appears to be retrograde its influence is diminished and/or modified. When it seems stationary its influence is considered to be strengthened.

The twelve signs cover the Earth's annual motion around the Sun and indicate function. As well as characterising signs by element (see Table following) in groups of three they can also be united in groups of four. These groups are the signs' qualities (or quadruplicities). Thus Aries, Cancer, Libra and Capricorn are all Cardinal signs. The Table shows the qualities of all the signs at a glance. Cardinal signs tend to be outgoing, fixed signs are resistant to change and mutable ones are adaptable. Alternating signs starting with Aries are considered to be positive (self-expressive) whereas those immediately after, starting with Taurus, are negative and tend to be more introvert. When a sign contains a planet the principle of that planet will be expressed in the manner of that sign. Thus we can interpret Mercury in Aries simply as "communication will be expressed assertively". Planets whose principles work best in certain signs, or show their finest principles most effectively, rule those signs, or become exalted in them, respectively. Conversely, when contained in signs opposite to these, they are considered to be in their detriment, or fall, as their principles are not very compatible in these signs. A planet placed in a sign ruled by another planet is ruled by that planet, and this is known as "disposition".

Name	Symbol	Meaning	Quality	Element	Manner	Ruler	Exaltation
Aries	♈	Ram	Cardinal	Fire	Assertively	Mars	Sun
Taurus	♉	Bull	Fixed	Earth	Possessively	Venus	Moon
Gemini	♊	Twins	Mutable	Air	Communica-tively	Mercury	Dragon's head
Cancer	♋	Crab	Cardinal	Water	Sensitively	Moon	Jupiter
Leo	♌	Lion	Fixed	Fire	Creatively	Sun	Neptune
Virgo	♍	Virgin	Mutable	Earth	Critically	Mercury	Mercury
Libra	♎	Scales	Cardinal	Air	Harmoniously	Venus	Saturn
Scorpio	♏	Scorpion	Fixed	Water	Passionately	Pluto	Uranus
Sagit-tarius	♐	Archer	Mutable	Fire	Widely, Deeply.	Jupiter	Dragon's tail
Capri-corn	♑	Goat	Cardinal	Earth	Prudently	Saturn	Mars

Aqua-rius	♒	Water-Carrier	Fixed	Air	Scientifically	Uranus	Chiron
Pisces	♓	Fishes	Mutable	Water	Appreciatively	Neptune	Venus

Possibly Chiron is a co-ruler of Virgo.

Each sign consists of thirty zodiacal degrees and so is easily subdivided into three equal decanates of ten degrees. The first decanate is considered to be more of the true nature of the sign whereas the second is influenced by the following sign in that element and the third one by the remaining sign in the element. Thus the second decanate of Aries is influenced by Leo and the third by Sagittarius. In this case the decanate sub-rulers are the Sun for Leo and Jupiter for Sagittarius respectively.

- -

CHAPTER 2

Great Circles and the Morinus System of Houses.

Inside a planetarium, imagining that we are seated at the Earth's centre, we can look up at the domed ceiling of stars above us, and at the same time, imagine the continuation to another dome of stars beneath us. This whole sky of stars that surrounds us is called the Celestial Sphere.

Diagram 1: The Celestial Sphere (described for Polar Elevation of 53 25'N, the Latitude for Liverpool.)

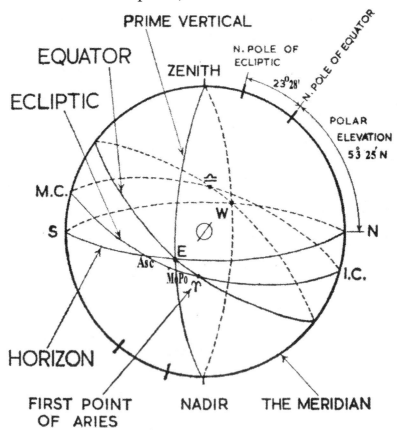

The plane of any circle that contains the centre of the Earth at its centre is called a Great circle. For example the Equator is a Great circle and corresponds to latitude 0⁰. All other circles of latitude, parallel to the Equator, but whose plane cannot contain the Earth's centre, are small circles. On the other hand, if we think about it for a moment, all circles of longitude are indeed Great circles.

Diagram 1 shows the major Great circles of the Celestial Sphere[8]. Probably the Meridian is the most important Great circle. It is the North – South Great circle and it passes through the North and South poles of the Equator, the North and South poles of the Ecliptic, the North and South points of the true Horizon, as well as the zenith and nadir (the poles of the true Horizon). The Sun crosses the Meridian at midday (anywhere on Earth) and this point of intersection with the Ecliptic (the Sun's apparent path and the circle of the Zodiac) is known as the Midheaven. We can speak of three other Great circles: the Prime Vertical, the Equator and the true Horizon, as secondaries to the Meridian because they all pass through the East – West points, the poles of the Meridian. The true Horizon must not be confused with the visible horizon, formed by the apparent meeting of the Earth with the sky, which is a small circle that is parallel to the true Horizon.

The Morinus House System.

Keeping our introduction of Great circles in mind we can construct our own personal map of the Zodiac, containing the heavenly bodies of the Solar System (even the Sun and Moon are considered to be "planets" of the Earth as far as Astrology is concerned – remember that the Earth is geocentric!) This is a picture/chart of the heavens as they appeared at the time and place of our birth on Earth. Nowadays we can do this easily using a computer and the appropriate software. Briefly, the first step in making/casting/erecting the chart is to calculate our Star (sidereal) time of birth, unlike clock time, that is determined by the Sun. Anyone can do this by means of a very simple formula. The second step is to calculate the twelve "Houses of Heaven". Houses are different from Signs and should not be confused with them. The Signs come from dividing the apparent, circular path of the Sun around the earth once a year, by twelve. However, the Houses derive from dividing by twelve the apparent, circular path the heavens make around the Earth every day (due to the Earth's spin). Thus Signs come from the yearly cycle and the Houses from the daily cycle. By superimposing these two cycles on one another, with the Earth at the common centre, we construct a chart of the heavens for each of our birth times. Thirdly, we use an ephemeris (regular data files of the positions of the Sun, Moon and planets) to put the planets in the Zodiac, and finally list the various aspects (angles) they make with the Earth among themselves. Note, however, that there are in fact several different ways of making the twelve-fold division of the Zodiac into Houses. These methods all have their supporters and detractors but the method that we shall use was devised by the great French astrologer and mathematician, Morin de Villefranche, known as Morinus. His astrological logic proceeded as follows:

Our Earth itself is defined by the Equator with its axis passing through the North and South poles. At our moment of birth we can fix the position of our Houses by seeing where the Meridian and the true Horizon intersect the Equator. We trisect the quadrant so formed so that, with all four quadrants we now have twelve equidistant points around the Equator. We take these points as centres (rather than the boundaries) of the Houses, thus making them more symmetrical about the place of birth.

To specify House centres in terms of the heavens we now have to apply the sky to the Earth. We define the sky by the Ecliptic (the Zodiac), the yearly apparent path of the Sun around the Earth, with its axis passing through its own North and South poles. The points where six Great circles, each passing through the North and South poles of the Ecliptic, and through two different and opposite House centre points on the Equator, describe the House centres in terms of degrees of the Zodiac (see diagram 2). In other words House centres on the Equator are determined as "celestial longitude". Essentially, this is the House system proposed by Morinus. The first House centre, called the Morin point, is the East point (i.e. the point of intersection of the true Horizon with the Equator) projected onto the Ecliptic. In a sense it is a triple E point, where the East point of the Horizon on the Equator is defined by the Ecliptic. The Morin point is at right angles (orthogonal) to the Midheaven*.

<u>Diagram 2:</u> The Morinus House System and its House Boundaries at Birth+.

---------- House Boundaries

- - - - - Angular House Centres

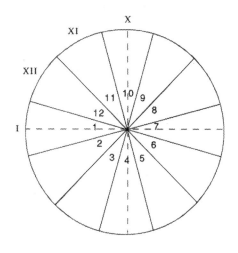

Figure 1 Distribution of House Boundaries About the Place of Birth

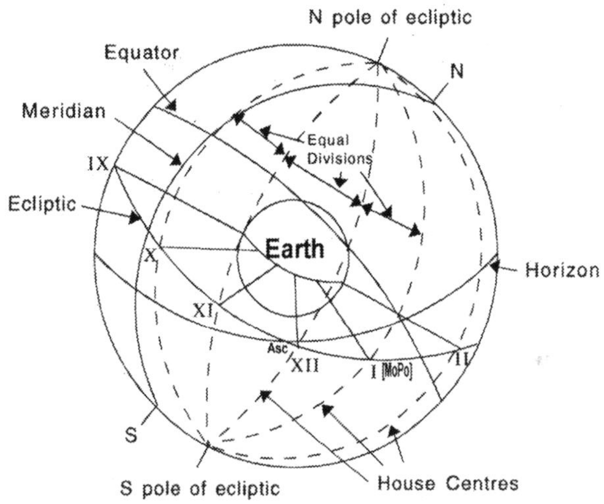

Figure 2 The Morinus House System[3]

The twelve Houses chart the Earth's daily motion and describe our Earthly experience or "circumstances".

House Number	Description	Experience
1st	Angular	The Person, Personality
2nd	Succedent	Resource, Money, Feelings, Possessions.
3rd	Cadent	Brethren, Communications, Neighbours.
4th	Angular	Home, House, End of Life, Parent at Home.
5th	Succedent	Pleasures, Love, Children, Self-expression.

6th	Cadent	Service in work. Health.
7th	Angular	Partnerships, Competitors, Opportunity.
8th	Succedent	Legacies, Regeneration, Life-force, Death.
9th	Cadent	Understanding, Religion, Profound interests.
10th	Angular	Public standing, Profession, Working parent.
11th	Succedent	Friends, Hopes, Objectives
12th	Cadent	Retirement, Escape, Sacrifice, The Subconscious.

Angular Houses indicate present circumstances and tend to impart initiative. Succedent Houses suggest future situations and resultant status, whereas Cadent Houses show previously established situations as well as dispersed ideas and energies.

- -

CHAPTER 3

Chart Shaping and Interplanetary Aspect Patterns

<u>Overall Chart Shaping:</u> If most of the planets lie to the East in a chart then the interpretation is that destiny is in the person's hands. If they lie to the West predominantly then the person's destiny is in others' hands or dependent on prevailing conditions. If most of the planets lie above the horizon (i.e. in the top half of the chart) then the interpretation is that the person is objective. Conversely, if they lie mostly below the horizon (i.e. in the bottom half of the chart) then the interpretation is that the person is largely subjective. More specifically, the interpretation of the actual overall shaping of a chart has been regarded only relatively recently[8]. Seven basic types occur:

<u>The Splash.</u> The planets are scattered around the chart. At best this means a genuine, universal width of interest, or, at worst, one who scatters his interests too much.

<u>The Bundle.</u> All the planets are concentrated within a third of a chart. This indicates that the course of the life is restricted within certain narrow bands of opportunity; i.e. one who is inhibited compared, say, with a 'Splash' type person.

<u>The Locomotive.</u> The reverse of the 'Bundle' in that all the planets are confined within two thirds of a chart, leaving the remaining third empty. Here the temperament drives forwards; the important planet is that leading in a clockwise direction towards the empty third and is judged by the House which it occupies.

<u>The Bowl.</u> All the planets lie in one half of the chart. If the division is along the horizon, or along the meridian line, a hemisphere of influence is formed. The 'Bowl' type holds something and is self-contained in that the person is cut off from the other hemisphere of experience. The person seeks to capture that experience and give it

to his fellows, either constructively or vindictively. This type of person tends to be idealistic.

<u>The Bucket.</u> All the planets but one lie in one hemisphere. This one constitutes the 'Bucket's' handle. When it is alone, either above the horizon or below, or either to the East or to the West, then it is known as a 'singleton' and reveals an important direction of interest. A 'Bucket' shaping indicates a rather uncompromising direction to the life-effort.

<u>The See-Saw.</u> The planets lie in two groups, roughly opposed to each other across the chart. The person's tendency here is to act at all times under a consideration of opposing views, or under a sensitiveness to contrasting possibilities, i.e. the person tends to be indecisive, but choices finally made will have been well-considered.

<u>The Splay.</u> The planets cluster together in strong and sharp aggregations at irregular points around the chart. This generates an individualistic temperament that robustly resists pigeon-holing.

<u>Aspects</u> are specific angles (i.e. the Zodiac circle of 360^0 divided by successive whole numbers starting with one) subtended at the centre of the Earth (geocentric) between two planets. They are measured in degrees around the Zodiac (Ecliptic). For example, division of 360^0 by one gives us 360^0, which brings us back to where we started from on the circle and is equivalent to 0^0, i.e. the conjunction. Division by two gives us 180^0 and places us diametrically across the ecliptic circle from our starting point so giving us the opposition. Similarly, division by three gives us 120^0, giving us the trine, and division by four gives us the square, an aspect of 90^0, and so on.

There are five major aspects and several minor ones:

Major Aspect Name	Angular Distance around Ecliptic.	Aspect Orb	Symbol	Nature
CONJUNCTION	0^0	8^0	☌	Variable

OPPOSITION	180^0	8^0	☍	Difficult
TRINE	120^0	8^0	△	Easy
SQUARE	90^0	8^0	□	Difficult
SEXTILE	60^0	4^0	✳	Easy

Minor Aspect Family Name	Angular Distance around Ecliptice	Aspect Orb	Symbol	Nature
Quintile	72^0, 1440	2^0	Q, Q2	Intelligence
Septile	51^0 26', 102^0 54' 154^0 18'.	2^0	S, S2,S3	Independence
Semi Square	45^0	2^0	∠	Difficult
Sesquiquadrate	135^0	2^0	⊡	Difficult
Nonile	40^0, 80^0, 160^0.	2^0	N, N2,N4	Easy
Decile	36^0, 108^0.	2^0	D, D3	Intelligence
Undecile	32^0 43' etc.	2^0	U, U2 etc.	Gentility
Semi-sextile	30^0	2^0	⊻	Easy
Quincunx	150^0	2^0	⊼	Difficult

Their interpretation is all important because it qualifies the way in which the principles of the planets manifest. Thus the meaning of every aspect is 'two-way'. Aspects to the Ruler, Sun or Moon are usually more important. Additionally other aspects to two aspecting planets modify the interpretation of the original aspect. Aspects not only unite planets, they emphasise the sign (if conjunction), the element (if trine) and the quality (if opposition or square) in which it functions. Traditionally they were described as good or bad, or evil but now words such as easy and difficult are preferred. The nature of an aspect depends on the planets making up the aspect. Venus and Jupiter tend to be beneficial/easy whereas Saturn and Mars make the aspects difficult. An exact aspect is very much stronger than a wide one. The extreme width of its action is called its 'orb' i.e. the Orb of an aspect is the distance of separation permitted by the planets while in aspect.   Additional considerations include the absence of aspects to a planet (its principle is then not well co-ordinated with the rest of the personality) and aspects between two planets that are not aspected by any of the others (the personality may then seem to be divided or split).   When two planets, not in proper aspect to each other, are both aspected by a third, this other may bring them into aspect by "translation of light".   When each of two planets is found to be in the sign ruled by the other they are brought into a relationship as if they were in conjunction.   This is called "Mutual Reception".   A planet moving towards exactness of aspect with another is said to be "applying" and so strengthening, whereas if it is moving away then it is called "separating" and so weakening.   If two planets are equidistant from the celestial equator, either to its North or to its South, or both, then they are said to be in "Parallel of Declination", symbol P, with an orb of 1^0.   If on the same side of the Earth then P has the property of the conjunction but if on the opposite side then P's property is of the opposition.   Ps are very rarely used.   'Undeciles' (the ecliptic divided by eleven) are not used at all.

Pelletier[3] has published a whole book of interpretations based on the House positions of aspecting planets.   These have proved both useful and valid.

Specific Interplanetary Aspect Patterns. Presently there are six main groups of these:

T-Square. The tenseness of an opposition will be aggravated when another planet is square to both ends of the opposition (bi-square). Usually a T-Square is of the cardinal, fixed or mutable quality.   The short arm of the T (or the bi-square planet) gives the T-Square its focus.   On the other hand the tenseness will be eased if another planet is trine to one end of the opposition and at the same time sextile to the other. This is called mediation.

Grand Trine.   The ease of working of an element (fire, earth, air, water) is intensified when three or more planets complete an equilateral triangle in the chart.   Sometimes the ease produced can lead some persons to become "parasitical".

Grand Cross.   Difficulty is raised to an optimum when four or more planets complete a four-cornered square that will simultaneously contain two oppositions.   Charts containing this pattern should be examined for mediation, e.g. the presence of an easing aspect to one of the four corners.   Crosses formed in different qualities are different in effect.   Thus a Cardinal cross implies an intention to surmount difficulties, a Fixed one to put up with them and a Mutable one to by-pass them but all of these lead to resultant strain for the person.

Yod – The Finger of God.   The pattern of two planets in close sextile, with a third in quincunx to both, is called a Yod.   This suggests opportunities that the person seemingly is compelled to take up, for better or worse, depending on the rest of the chart.   There is always transformation contained in the basic working out of the Yod.   As we can imagine there are other triangular patterns similar to the Yod. For example, two planets in close square, with a third that is sesquiquadrate to both; or two planets in close quintile with a third that is biquintile to both.   Interpretations for these will be different from those of the Yod.

Bi-Aspect patterns.   A third planet at a specific midpoint between two others tends to form meaningful triangles.   Such planets are said to be bi-an aspect, such as bi-sextile (at the midpoint of a trine); bi-semisextile (at the midpoint of a sextile) and bi-semisquare (at the midpoint of a square).

Kites.   The starting condition for a kite is an opposition that is then flanked equidistantly and specifically, on either side, by other planets.   Thus a Grand Cross is one extreme form of kite that contains optimum strain.   At the other extreme, one planet opposing a closely gathered group of planets (i.e. a stellium) across a chart produces a fanhandle. If we find a Grand Trine with an extra planet that is bi-sextile on one side then this planet will oppose the remaining planet(s) across the chart and so we form a Grand Trine Kite. This is the kite that contains the greatest amount of ease. Similarly, if we take a Yod and find an extra planet that is bi-semisextile to those forming the sextile we see that it will also oppose the remaining planet that is quincunx to both those forming the sextile. This kite contains considerable strain. Kites based on the quintile and decile families probably also contain significant strain. The Table summarises the presently accepted types of possible kites.

Kite Name	Family	Angle subtended at the Earth by the short cross-bar.	Influence
Fanhandle	Conjunction	Essentially 0^0	Strain
Quincunx (Yod)	Dodecile	60^0	Strain + Ease
Biquintile	Decile	72^0	Neutral + Strain
Sesquiquadrate	Octile	90^0	Increased Strain
Trine (Grand)	Sextile	120^0	More Ease than Strain
Tredecile	Quintile	144^0	Neutral + Strain
Square (Grand +)	Quadruplicity	180^0	Optimum Strain

The meaning of a kite, in general, is that the principles of the planets comprising the kite will all be well-integrated within the character of the person involved. Notice that all kites contain innate strain due to the opposition produced by the kite's long cross-bar. The amount of strain is then modified by the nature of the other aspects making-up the kite as shown in the Table. Relief or aggravation of strain can also be achieved by external easing or straining aspects to the ends of the cross-bars. The main focus of a kite occurs at the sharp end apart from a Grand Cross kite, which doesn't have a sharp end; we then need other factors to help us to decide the focus of this kind of kite (e.g. Sun, Moon or Ruler, or that planet at the MoPo or M.C.).

Three Other Common Factors:

☊ The Dragon's head (Moon's Ascending Node) is a point of general "protection".

☋ The Dragon's tail (Moon's Descending Node) is a point of general "self-undoing".

⊕ The Part of Fortune (Morin Point – The Moon + the Sun) is a point of general "self-interest".

- -

References:

1) "The Pre-Natal Epoch", E. H. Bailey, Samuel Weiser, New York, USA, 1974.

2) A. Leo, "Astrology for All", Samuel Weiser, New York, U.S.A., 1978.

3) R. Pelletier, "Planets in Houses" and "Planets in Aspect", Para research Inc., Rockport, Mass., U.S.A., 1978 and 1974.

4) "The Modern Textbook of Astrology", M. E. Hone, L. N. Fowler, Romford, UK, Rev. Ed., 1978.

5) "The Cosmic Influence", F. King, Aldus Books, London, 1976.

6) "How to Judge a Nativity", A. Leo, L. N. Fowler, London, 1969.

7) "Astrology – How to Cast your Horoscope", R.C. Davison, Granada Publishing, 1979, London, U.K.

8) "The Guide to Horoscope Interpretation", M. E. Jones, The Theosophical Publishing House, Wheaton, Illinois, U.S.A., 1974.

9) "How to Learn Astrology", M. E. Jones, Routledge & Kegan Paul Ltd., London, 1977.

10) The Internet, Wikipedia, King Edward III of England.

11) The Oxford Dictionary of National Biography, 8159, 2007, the Internet.

12) "Karmic Astrology. Vols. 1 – 4", M. Schulman, The Aquarian Press, Wellingborough, U.K., 1978-9.

13) "Astrology: How and Why It Works", M. E. Jones, Routledge and Kegan Paul Ltd., London, 1977.

14) "Our Birth on Earth", C. Stubbs, Trafford Publishing, Bloomington, Indiana, U.S.A., 2009.

15) All astrological charts were obtained using "Solar Fire DeLuxe" software supplied by Esoteric Technologies (Astrolabe) Inc., Brewster, Maryland, U.S.A.

16) "1001 Notable Nativities", A. Leo, L. N. Fowler, London, U.K., 1917.

- -

CHAPTER 4

The Pre-Natal Epoch and the Ideal Birth Moment

"The only reliable method of rectification"

Ancient teaching tells us that the Moon is the chief controller of human generation. Concerning our individual origins there are two moments, that of birth and that of fertilisation, that are important astrologically. The only astrological rules that come anywhere close to fitting the modern, genetic description of the birth process belong to the "Trutine of Hermes". These were developed primarily by Sepharial (W. Gorn-Old) and published in book form by Bailey as "The Pre-Natal Epoch" in 1916. The rules contain four variables: i.e. the sex of the baby-to-be, and the positions of the Moon, of the Ascendant and, to a lesser extent, of the Sun. The only one of these about which we can have any reasonable doubt is that of the Ascendant. From experience there was difficulty using the Pre-Natal Epoch with the traditional Ascendant. Briefly, there appeared to be far too many either short or long term births when compared to the usual distribution of gestation periods around 273 days. Using the Morin Point instead seemed to restore the expected distribution.

The rules state (but substituting the Morin Point for the Ascendant):

1) When the Moon at Birth is increasing in light (i.e. going from the new to the full Moon) it will be the Morin Point at Epoch, and the Moon at Epoch will be the Morin Point at Birth.

2) When the Moon at Birth is decreasing in light (i.e. going from the full to the new Moon) it will be the point opposite the Morin Point at Epoch, and the Moon at Epoch will be the point opposite the Morin Point at Birth.

These are extended by two further rules:

3)   When the Moon at Birth is increasing in light and below the Morin Point, or when decreasing in light and above the Morin Point, then the period of gestation will be longer than the average.

4) When the Moon at Birth is increasing in light and above the Morin Point, or when decreasing in light and below the Morin Point, then the period of gestation will be shorter than the average.

   From these four laws we can define Four Orders of Regular Epochs as follows in the Table:

Order	Condition	Period of Gestation
1	Moon above and increasing	273 days – x
2	Moon above and decreasing	273 days + x
3	Moon below and increasing	273 days + x
4	Moon below and decreasing	273 days – x

- -

273 days corresponds to the normal period of gestation (ten cycles of the Moon) counted backwards from the date of birth and gives the "Index date". x is the number of days equivalent to the number of degrees of the Moon with respect to the Morin Point, or to its opposite, at birth, depending on the Order number, divided by 13. (On average the Moon travels 13^0 per day around the ecliptic [Zodiac]). + or – x days from the Index date then gives the "Epoch date". There then follow three sex rules governing the positions of the Moon and of the Morin Point (both at Epoch) that allow us to determine the sex of the baby-to-be. Bailey's Table gives us the sex, or non-sex, of all the degrees of the Zodiac.

For the Epochal chart:

1) When the Morin Point is negative (non-sex), as in strict regular and irregular epochs, the sex of the position occupied by the Moon will be the sex of the baby-to-be.

2) When the Moon and the Morin Point positions are within orbs of degrees of the same sex, the sex of the baby-to-be is the same as the positions so occupied.

3) When the Moon and the Morin Point positions are placed within orbs of degrees of the opposite sex – the Moon in a female position and the Morin Point in a male position, or vice-versa – the sex of the baby-to-be is determined by the sex of the quadrant containing the Moon.

The sex of a baby-to-be is decided at its moment of fertilisation by the invading sperm. In practice, and almost without exception, we know the sex of the child, and then we must find an Epoch that agrees with this.

The rules show that at the Pre-Natal Epoch (moment of fertilisation) there is a particular configuration of the heavens (mainly the Moon, but also the Sun) with respect to the Earth (Morin Point). It then follows, some nine months (ten cycles of the Moon) later, that there will be a related configuration of the heavens occurring at what we can call "The Ideal Birth Moment".

Bailey's Sex Quadrants are given in the following diagram:

BAILEY'S SEX QUODRANTS

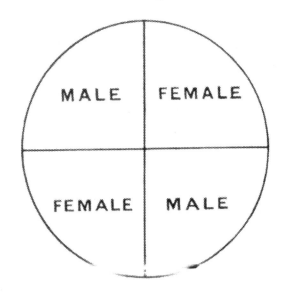

S.E. (Meridian to Morin Point) and N.W. quadrants are male and N.E. (Meridian to opposite to the Morin Point) and S.W. quadrants are female. . Notice how well they fit in with the Morinus House System.

BAILEY'S TABLE OF SEX DEGREES

Sex.	Limits of		Exact Sex Point.	Limits of	
	Moon's Orb.	Morin Pt's Orb.		Morin Pt's Orb.	Moon's Orb.
F	—	—	♈ 0.0	♈ 4.17	♈ 6.26
M	♈ 6.26	♈ 8.34	♈ 12.51	♈ 17.9	♈ 19.17
M	♈ 19.17	♈ 21.26	♈ 25.43	♉ 0.0	♉ 2.9
F	♉ 2.9	♉ 4.17	♉ 8.34	♉ 12.51	♉ 15.0
M	♉ 15.0	♉ 17.9	♉ 21.26	♉ 25.43	♉ 27.51
F	♉ 27.51	♊ 0.0	♊ 4.17	♊ 8.34	♊ 10.43
F	♊ 10.43	♊ 12.51	♊ 17.9	♊ 21.26	♊ 23.34
F	♊ 23.34	♊ 25.43	♋ 0.0	♋ 4.17	♋ 6.26
F	♋ 6.26	♋ 8.34	♋ 12.51	♋ 17.9	♋ 19.17
M	♋ 19.17	♋ 21.26	♋ 25.43	♌ 0.0	♌ 2.9
M	♌ 2.9	♌ 4.17	♌ 8.34	♌ 12.51	♌ 15.0
M	♌ 15.0	♌ 17.9	♌ 21.26	♌ 25.43	♌ 27.51
M	♌ 27.51	♍ 0.0	♍ 4.17	♍ 8.34	♍ 10.43
F	♍ 10.43	♍ 12.51	♍ 17.9	♍ 21.26	♍ 23.34
M	♍ 23.34	♍ 25.43	♎ 0.0	♎ 4.17	♎ 6.26
F	♎ 6.26	♎ 8.34	♎ 12.51	♎ 17.9	♎ 19.17
F	♎ 19.17	♎ 21.26	♎ 25.43	♏ 0.0	♏ 2.9
M	♏ 2.9	♏ 4.17	♏ 8.34	♏ 12.51	♏ 15.0
F	♏ 15.0	♏ 17.9	♏ 21.26	♏ 25.43	♏ 27.51
M	♏ 27.51	♐ 0.0	♐ 4.17	♐ 8.34	♐ 10.43
M	♐ 10.43	♐ 12.51	♐ 17.9	♐ 21.26	♐ 23.34
M	♐ 23.34	♐ 25.43	♑ 0.0	♑ 4.17	♑ 6.26
M	♑ 6.26	♑ 8.34	♑ 12.51	♑ 17.9	♑ 19.17
F	♑ 19.17	♑ 21.26	♑ 25.43	♒ 0.0	♒ 2.9
F	♒ 2.9	♒ 4.17	♒ 8.34	♒ 12.51	♒ 15.0
F	♒ 15.0	♒ 17.9	♒ 21.26	♒ 25.43	♒ 27.51
F	♒ 27.51	♓ 0.0	♓ 4.17	♓ 8.34	♓ 10.43
M	♓ 10.43	♓ 12.51	♓ 17.9	♓ 21.26	♓ 23.34
F	♓ 23.34	♓ 25.43	♓ 30.0	—	—

EXPLANATION.—Column 4 of the table shows the exact sex point. Cols 3 and 5 show where the influence of the Morin Pt. commences and finishes respectively. Cols. 2 and 6 show where the moon's influence commences and finishes respectively. Col. 1 gives the sex of the area between the longitudes in Cols. 2 and 6.

EXAMPLE.— Morin Pt at epoch, Cancer 18° 5'. Moon, Scorpio 15° 24'. Looking down the columns headed "Morin Pt.'s Orb," it will be seen that Cancer 18° 5' is outside the limits given. It is, therefore, negative. Looking down the columns headed "Moon's Orb," it will be seen that Scorpio 15° commences a male area, and the moon will therefore be in an area of that sex. The same rule applies to all cases.

CHAPTER 5

Interpretations

"DNA consists of two long strands along which genetic material is bonded regularly. The strands run in opposite directions and are entwined like vines in the form of a double helix. The genetic material holds the strands together tightly."

"Not only do we derive our physical form
but also our character from our genes."

"There is a wholeness about a Birth, or an Epoch, horoscope
but a completeness when these are combined."

"The idea of duality is the nature of human experience."
M. Shulman[11]

Previously we saw that in all likelihood we derive our character from our genes[14]. These become established at our Moment of Fertilisation (The Pre-Natal Epoch). Traditionally we determine our astrological character by interpreting the indicators present in our Birth charts but we shall now recommend that it should be based for a substantial part on our Epoch charts as well. Bailey said that the Epoch (fertilisation) time shows the inherent character of the new individual about to manifest in the flesh whereas the Birth time denotes the actual, personal conditions into which the individual is born.

The first assumption we shall make is that we can use interpretations of indicators for the Epoch chart in just the same way, and just as well as normally for the Birth chart. Secondly we shall assume that interpretations for the Epoch chart will have equal weighting with those of the Birth chart. The rules of the Pre-Natal Epoch clearly specify the relationships between the Morin Points and the positions of the Moon at Epoch and at Birth. For all of the book's Power Notables we shall note the order and type of their Epochs, and indicate the positions of the Sun, Moon and Morin Point for each of their Epoch and Birth charts together with their respective interpretations.

We look to notables to examine their characters, successes and even failures in order to try and conduct our own lives more successfully and also to avoid obvious mistakes. If we can appreciate what it was that made people famous then we can apply this appreciation to our own characters (both strengths and weaknesses), relationships, careers and health and this will then enable us to decide what suits us best. Carrying out this exercise effectively constitutes one of the main challenges for Astrology. Our proposal in this book is that we can do a much better job by considering a combination of the interpretations of both sets of indicators of our Epoch and Birth charts rather than just using either one of them separately. We shall try to justify this combination by interpreting the Epoch and Birth charts of famous people and then include within the combined and synthesised result recent biographical material, supplemented by, for example, material from articles in encyclopaedias such as Wikipedia.

Character traits exist only in the abstract, in the domain of Psychology, as a branch of the Behavioural/Social Sciences that lie at the edge of the scope of science. They are qualitative, rather than quantitative, terms. Please note that none of the character interpretations within the book is mine; I have simply taken the interpretation of the various indicators (see the Appendices) from several standard texts (see the References at the end of Chapter 3) and have tried to blend them into a readily understandable whole.

In this way the interpretations used are impartial, objective and so more scientific. This means that they are free from hero myths, personality cults, exaggerations, and image polishing. Additionally, since the problems involved in trying to extract impartial truth from ancient and medieval biographical material are legion, we dispense with these as well. On the other hand, astrological interpretations tend to lack accuracy and so standardisation by their very nature. Moreover, these interpretations depend strongly upon the accuracy of the birth data available and in turn on the indicators on which they are based. Possibly a combination of both approaches could lead to more realistic biographies.

Fortunately, humans are very good at making comparisons between two different people so long as the person making the comparison is not one of those involved. The general idea is for the reader to judge if the combined interpretation of the charts for each power notable describes that particular notable alone and does not fit any of the other power notables also presented in the book. The reader should be able to do this easily.

We could carry out our method for producing horoscope interpretations at two levels. Firstly we could use a full-blown set of interpretations of indicators but alternatively, and more practically, we can create a relevant Person Summary that will cover most of the known characteristics of a person that should suffice for our purposes. These Person Summaries are interspersed with referenced biographical extracts, inserted relevantly, between brackets or apostrophes. The indicators used (at both Birth and Epoch) for assembling a Person Summary comprise:

1) Overall Chart Shaping[8].
2) Special Interplanetary Aspect Patterns[8, 9].
3) Sun and Moon Sign combination[2].
4) Sun and Moon House combination[3].
5) Strongest Aspects to the Sun and Moon[4] only.

6)   Morin Point Sign[4] and Decanate[6].

7)   Chart Ruler in Sign, House and the strongest aspects it[6, 7] receives

8)   Rising Planets[4] and Retrograde Personal Planets[11]

If we should wish to extend this set of indicators to create a full description of combined interpretations then we could also include:

1)   Planetary sign synthesis[4].

2)   Angular, succedent and cadent planetary totals[4].

3)   Remaining planets such as Venus and Mars and their aspects[3].

4)   Positive and negative planet totals[4].

5)   Unaspected planets[4].

6)   Other Retrograde planets[4, 11].

7)   Rulerships, Exaltations and Mutual Receptions[4, 6, 8].

8)   Detriments and Falls[4, 6, 8].

9)   Part of Fortune[4, 11] (Morin Point + Moon – Sun).

10) Dragon's Head[4, 11] (Moon's Node).

11) Parallels of Declination[4] (both conjunction and opposition).

   We need to be aware of these added indicators for Person Summaries.

- -

   Now we are ready to examine our first Power Notable, namely King Edward III of England.

CHAPTER 6

King Edward III of England

"The Greatest General in English History."

King Edward the third (KEIII) was one of the most successful monarchs of the Middle Ages.   Restoring royal authority after the disastrous reign of his father (KEII), he went on to transform England into the most efficient military power in Europe.   KEIII's reign saw vital developments in legislature, government and especially the evolution of the English parliament..   The ravages of the Black Death occurred during his reign, which lasted for fifty years.

Edward III was crowned at the age of fourteen following his father's abdication.   At age seventeen he led a coup against his regent, Roger Mortimer.   After defeating, but not subjugating, Scotland, he declared himself the rightful heir to the French throne in 1340, thereby starting the Hundred Years' War.   After some initial setbacks the war went exceptionally well for England; the victories of Sluys, Crécy, Poitiers and the capture of Calais, led to the highly favourable Treaty of Brétigny.   However, KEIII's later years were marked by international failure and domestic strife due largely to his inertia and eventual bad health.

KEIII was a temperamental man, but also capable of great clemency.   He was mostly conventional, mainly interested in warfare and became highly revered in his own lifetime and later.   Although he was denounced by Whig historians, their view has been superceded and modern biographers credit him with remarkable achievements.

Figure 1: Epoch Chart and Aspect Grid for King Edward III.

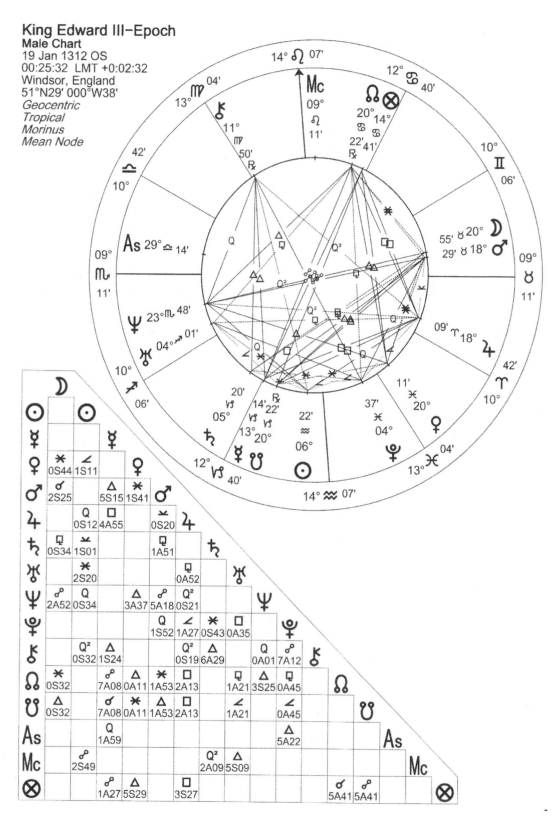

King Edward III – Horoscopes

KEIII was born at 5:30 a.m. on the 13th November, 1312 OS, at Windsor, England. His Epoch* occurred on the 19th January, 1312 at 0:25 a.m. Figure 1 shows his Epoch chart and aspect grid. We see that the planets lie mainly below the Earth (North), indicating a subjective nature, and that the overall shaping is a 'bucket' with Chiron in Virgo in the 11th House as the slightly anticlockwise handle planet across the Neptune opposition to the Mars – Moon conjunction; the rim of the bucket. This suggests that he gave and received practical and not uncritical support from his friends, which he in turn reciprocated. The bucket shaping suggests a particular and uncompromising direction to his life-effort. The Moon conjoint Mars in Taurus in the 7th House indicates a robust, courageous nature and the combined opposition to Neptune indicates great sensitivity but also a tendency towards reserve. Venus, exalted in Pisces, is sextile the Moon and trine Neptune thereby easing the strain in the Moon – Neptune opposition. Saturn lies in its own sign, Capricorn, suggesting steady control. Pluto (ruler) in Pisces, square Uranus and sextile Saturn is in mutual reception with Neptune in Scorpio. All this implies that his compassion and imagination were stimulated, that his financial resources would be fluctuating and that renunciation, in general, could become an obsession. The Sun in Aquarius – Moon in Taurus polarity gives true insight into human

- -

* At birth the Moon is below the Earth and increasing in light so that the Epoch will be 3rd Order. Both the Morin Point and the Moon occupy female areas showing that the Epoch will be a Sex one, of Type 4. Of the three possible Type 4 Epochs only the irregular, 3rd variation type gives rise to a valid Epoch for a male birth.

Figure 2: Birth Chart and Aspect Grid for King Edward III.

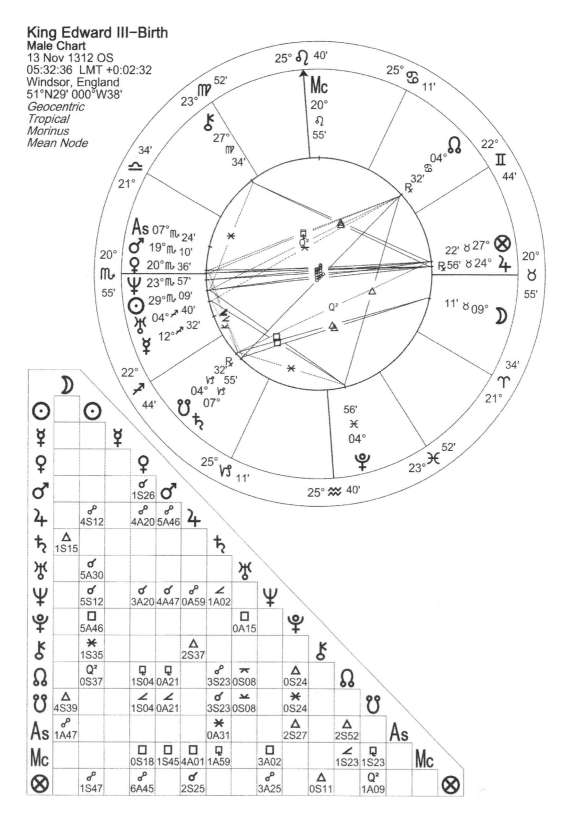

nature and suggests that he should take stock before marrying too soon. Notice also that this chart contains seven quintile family aspects that impart intelligence to the character.

The Epoch generates the Birth chart and aspect grid shown in Figure 2. Examination of this chart shows a See-Saw type shaping with a stellium of six planets, four of which lie in Scorpio, in the 1st House facing (opposite to) retrograde Jupiter in Taurus in the 7th House. The Eastern emphasis of the six planets means that KEIII's destiny is in his own hands, whereas the See-Saw shaping suggests the possibility of unique achievement through unexpected developments. The special kite interplanetary aspect pattern shown here is called a 'fanhandle' in which the focus is directed towards the retrograde Jupiter. Normally we should not consider Jupiter as a personal planet but for KEIII's Birth chart, because of the focus directed onto it, it does indeed become so. For KEIII it means that it is difficult for him to adapt himself to other people's way of thinking. It also means that he is able to see himself easily through the eyes of others. The opposition of Jupiter to Neptune suggests treachery. Oppositions to Jupiter are hardly very stressful (it is the great benefic) but what stress there may be is lessened by the trine to Chiron i.e. support from friends. The Sun – Moon polarities in Scorpio – Taurus and in the 1st House – 7th House reveal his love of display and how well he responds to challenges. The Morin point lies in the 3rd Scorpio decanate showing his desire for attachment and the attendant jealous tendencies. Pluto (ruler) in Pisces in the 4th House is square to Uranus showing the vital part played by negative and upsetting parental influence that forced him to assert himself and succeed on his own. Notice that Mercury in Sagittarius in the 2nd House is unaspected*, which means that his intellect is not well integrated with the rest of his personality. In this case his "far-flung" ideas may have had little to do with his overall nature.

Notice also that the Morin point for both KEIII's charts lies in Scorpio. In addition the position of the Moon in both charts lies in Taurus. This unusual, combined situation simplifies interpretation but also emphasises the importance of these two major indicators in his charts. Appendices 1a and 1b list the indicators and their interpretations for KEIII's Epoch and Birth charts respectively. The contents of these appendices were divided into four categories, namely character, relationships, career and health. The contents of each category were then organised into what is hoped is a reasonably understandable whole.

In the following Person Summary interpretations deriving from the Epoch chart are presented in normal type, those from the Birth chart in italics, whilst those interpretations common to both charts are presented in bold type. Inserted biographical extracts are enclosed either by apostrophes or by brackets.

- -

* In fact Mercury is in a separating pentaundecile (U⁵) (163⁰ 38') at a distance of 1⁰ 24' from exactness. This is hardly a strong, minor aspect and no attempt has been made to include any possible interpretation for this in KEIII's Person Summary. However, when all else is absent, whatever remains could well become significant. An interpretation for Mercury in the 2nd House in the 8th House position from Jupiter in the 7th House reads, "He was immediately aware when anyone tried to undermine him or to resort to unfair practices. He was willing to make sacrifices for the "right" person, whom he hoped would share his life, and no gift was too costly when he wanted to impress that person." Additionally, for this case, the situation of Mercury in his Epoch chart assumes more relevance. Here Mercury in the 3rd House is trine to Chiron in the 11th House and so is in the 5th House from it. The full interpretation for this is given in Appendix 1b showing that he was well-liked by his friends. Both of these interpretations seem to fit KEIII rather well!

Person Summary plus Biographical Extracts

Character

<u>General:</u> KEIII was highly dignified, self-controlled, robust and courageous in manner, **firm** sincere, just and reliable. *He had self-determination and the leverage of power.* **He was genial, warm, affectionate,** *generally good-natured,* (familiar and affable) cheerful and contented with his own surroundings. *Thus his forcefulness was softened.* *He had a great love of display* (feasts, tournaments, games, hunting and jousts) *and of management success* (he was delighted when his plans came to fruition but enraged when he was let down).

<u>Mentality:</u> He was intelligent, showed great sensitivity, prudence, **high imagination and compassion**, all of which led to true insight into human nature. *Thus he could read character well but had a tendency to be self-willed, dogmatic, rash* (impulsive), *quarrelsome, boastful, eccentric, explosive and even fanatical. His mentality was not well-integrated with the rest of his personality. For example, this means that his decisively expressed, "far-flung" ideas, his interest in acquiring languages* (he knew French, Spanish, Italian, Dutch as well as English) *and his money-making ways would have existed apart from his general nature. These facets of his personality needed to have been recognised as such and so treated with caution.*

<u>Lifestyle:</u> **At his worst he had a criminal personality seeking fulfilment of personal aims without regard for the feelings of others** (he sanctioned massacres, beheadings, village and land destruction, etc.). *It was the thrill of competition that made him accept challenges.* 'He had a passion for the challenges of kingship and so war; he wanted to defeat the Scots and the French, the latter against the prevailing odds.' *He thrived on sensationalism and conflict. Opportunities and "good-luck" were to be expected* (he escaped traps set for his army by King Philip VI of France). *He was restless and eager and when stimulated his aggressive nature sprang into action.* Indeed, he was over-active at times and over-quick to respond. He had a compelling need to achieve understanding

and concentrated much energy establishing that he was always right. This made it difficult for him to adapt himself to other people's way of thinking (he came to accept that generally he was wrong about the Archbishop of Canterbury). *He stubbornly held on to past concepts. His ego-problem related to unrealistic expectations from life. Although he needed to feel dominant, he argued to uphold a principle rather than for his own need to win. Accordingly he could become overly self-righteous. He learnt his greatest truths in the most natural way and only at times when he was not trying to impress others or to exert himself. He looked at himself as seen through the eyes of others and taught himself to stand for what he thought others would admire. He had to learn to balance the nature of truth through the many ways it is expressed from person to person in his life. He needed to learn that differences between right and wrong lie strictly in the mind of the individual. His general tendency was to act at all times under a consideration of opposing views or to sensitiveness to contrasting and antagonistic possibilities.* He dug deeply into life and poured forth the gathered materials of his experience with unremitting zeal. *It disturbed him to be ignored as he was much more sensitive than others realised. He always tried to be pleasant because he truly enjoyed people.* A strong mothering influence was always in the background of his consciousness. Later on, general renunciation became an obsession and he developed a tendency to retirement, to philanthropy and to day-dreaming.

Relationships

<u>Others:</u> *He was not always fortunate making decisions.* 'Thus John Molyns was a criminal and undeserving of pardon and the Black Prince was not suited to be Governor of Aquitaine.' He could not function well unless he was involved with people and most of his opportunities came from the social contacts he made. However, he was not sure that he could live up to their expectations of him. 'He was nervous – terrified even – of Mortimer, whom he both feared and admired.' *He was often overly impressed with his competitors' qualifications so he was less forceful*

than he should have been asserting himself and his talent (particularly with Mortimer when KEIII was young). *It was in response to the challenges and competition presented by others that eventually he would prove himself. He made certain concessions if he could in order to win others' support and approval in his climb to prominence. He experienced impatience in wanting to please others* but he had to be careful not to let others use him as a doormat ("Not master, but a slave to the lowest order," T. Walsingham). *His greatest danger lay in treachery and deception but he needed to check everyone's credentials and to believe only those facts that he could check* (he was let down by his allies in war, initially). His ability to perform was increased by avoiding getting too deeply involved with the people he dealt with. *Generally his social side and* his public relations *were well-developed.*

Friends: *He won friends and influenced people through his charm* (he was gracious). Usually he would wait for the other person to make the first move because he feared rejection or lack of interest. *However, once started, there was never a dull moment when he was around because he lent sparkle and wit to any gathering. He was well-liked by his friends because he didn't threaten their egos.* His need for companionship meant that he had to make many concessions to others. *He gave and accepted help from close friends. His wounded healer approach to them was carried out practically, critically and conservatively.*

Family: *The actions of his parents profoundly upset his young life.* 'Although he loved both parents and his mother in particular, in 1327 KEII had to abdicate in his son's favour and his mother had left his father for Roger Mortimer, the new Regent.' His strong family ties made it difficult for him to transfer his attention to other people *and so gain the independence he needed from family obligations* (to look after his father, his mother, and his wife, Philippa) *but he used his charm to avoid alienation.* His first task was to put his family into proper perspective to allow him to come and go as the demands of his career and social life required. 'From 1341 on he could be himself like never before [his fourteen years previously]. His saying, "It is as it is" was particularly enigmatic.' *His domestic side was well-developed.* Probably he enjoyed indulging his children (there were no rebellions later); he had a strong cherishing influence and this may have partly satisfied his hunger for attention.

<u>Lover:</u> *His ability to love and enjoy sexual life* (he had a compulsive need for his wife, Philippa, and later for Alice Perrers) *and all things of beauty was strong and robust but not so delicate. Possibly, in some ways, he was not so fortunate in marriage.* Probably his early training led him to believe that it was better to marry anyone than to remain single. With that attitude he could have ended up being single again! He should have postponed marrying until he was sure he wasn't trying to compensate for a poor parental image in his choice of a partner (KEII, his father, tried to warn him about this tendency) for such a situation would have proved unsatisfactory. He had to resist this urge to marry the first likely prospect (but he didn't, and he was lucky). *His need to be involved in partnership/marriage was an asset to him for his future plans* (Philippa gave him huge support and he lost his ambition after she died). *His partner had to be willing to share his enthusiasm for what he wanted to accomplish, which improved the quality of life for his family. Philippa may well have been overly self-righteous, too. If someone he loved, and who respected him, had a strong belief in his abilities then he would listen to them (e.g. Philippa and the burghers of Calais, also he listened to certain of his generals).*

Career

<u>Early:</u> *His destiny was in his own hands* (he donned armour, drew his sword and prepared to fight for his demands himself). *Private education supported his purposes, leading to involvement with large numbers of people from a position of authority* (tutored by Richard Bury). *He knew that careful planning was the best way to achieve his goals* (he became a successful diplomat as well as a military leader but also a cold

calculator, who followed long term plans). His frame of reference had to become increasingly intellectual rather than emotional to improve his ability to solve the many problems that arose. Being emotionally committed in his duties would have severely limited his effectiveness. **He could achieve honest success by resisting his criminal tendencies and by means of a thrusting, purposeful nature coupled with a capacity for hard work** (which he did). *Although restless in his birth place – the whole world was his home; he became completely involved with whatever world was around him* (as he showed in Flanders and France). *He achieved uniquely through unexpected developments* (militarily at the battles of Dopplin Moor and Halidon Hill) *but also had a tendency to waste energy by being out-of-touch with prevailing conditions* (his initial campaigns were not well-planned enough and he had to return to repeat them). *Challenge was the most stimulating condition for him and he literally glowed as he rose to the occasion.* 'He charged up and down to Scotland very quickly when needed.' *When situations became bogged down and he became bored/lost interest* (during sieges in Scotland and France), *he thrived on the many confrontations that he faced.* Sudden, impetuous decisions caused gains and losses but these were kept in bounds by his favourable self-control. *He needed legal advice even for insignificant agreements. He revived and successfully promoted chivalry that even by then had started to become a forgotten art but it suited his personal and regal needs* (for demonstration of kingship).

Middle: *He inherited great transformations* (partly from his grandfather, KEI). There was a particular and uncompromising direction to his life-effort (successful kingship) with no concern over end results, or of conserving either himself or his resources (enormously costly celebrations had to take place). It annoyed him to be without money (1338-1340 but he spent liberally anyway) but he had no excuse because his creative talent should have allowed him to increase his resources. He expected more from his efforts than he deserved because he didn't want to give up his indulgences (chivalry, etc.). He could have applied

carry it out. He lived in a groove all his life (his mission/idea of kingship). *His ultimate ambition was to gain full control over his circumstances.* He adapted his allegiances to lines along which he could make his effort count for the most. *He willingly accepted duty and success through orderly and practical ways even though these caused personal limitations and lack of gaiety.* He was an instructor and inspirer of others (particularly of his knights by creating the Order of the Garter). *Later he became interested in activities that brought him before the public* (lawmaker "to do right", parliament, large-scale builder, patron of the arts). *His sensitive understanding of human problems was helpful to him in his public services.*
<u>Late:</u> He patronised music, literature and art but really looked forward to the time when he could be free of daily harassment and effort. By using all his talent and resources he certainly realised that goal.

Health

He was of medium stature and physically strong (he wielded a huge sword). *There was a tendency to nervous disorders that were perhaps exacerbated by inner struggles.* Also, there was the possibility of paralysis (strokes?) and of accidents. Isolated circumstances were indicated at the end of his life (he died unlucky, miserable and alone)

Reference: "The Perfect King – The Life of Edward III, Father of the English Nation", Ian Mortimer, Pimlico, Random House Group, London, 2007.

- -

CHAPTER 7

Adolf Hitler

"What manner of man is this grim figure, who has performed these superb toils and loosed these frightful evils?"
Winston Churchill, *Great Contemporaries*.

Adolf Hitler was an Austrian-born German politician who became the leader of the Nazi party. He ruled Germany from 1933 – 1945 as Chancellor and Head of State (the Fuhrer). Decorated in WW1, Hitler joined the Nazi party in 1920, led it from 1921 but was imprisoned after a failed coup in 1923. He gained support by promoting nationalism, anti-Semitism and anti-communism using charismatic oratory and propaganda. As Fuhrer he pursued a foreign policy with the declared goal of seizing "living space" for Germany. His rebuilt Wehrmacht invaded Poland in 1939 causing the outbreak of WW2 in Europe. Within three years Germany and the Axis powers occupied most of Europe, large parts of Africa, East and South East Asia and the Pacific Ocean. However, the Allies gained the upper hand from 1942 onward and in 1945 invaded Germany from all sides. German forces committed numerous atrocities during WW2, in particular the systematic killing of about seventeen million civilians that included the genocide of around six million Jews, known as the holocaust.

Figure 3: Epoch Chart and Aspect Grid for Adolf Hitler.

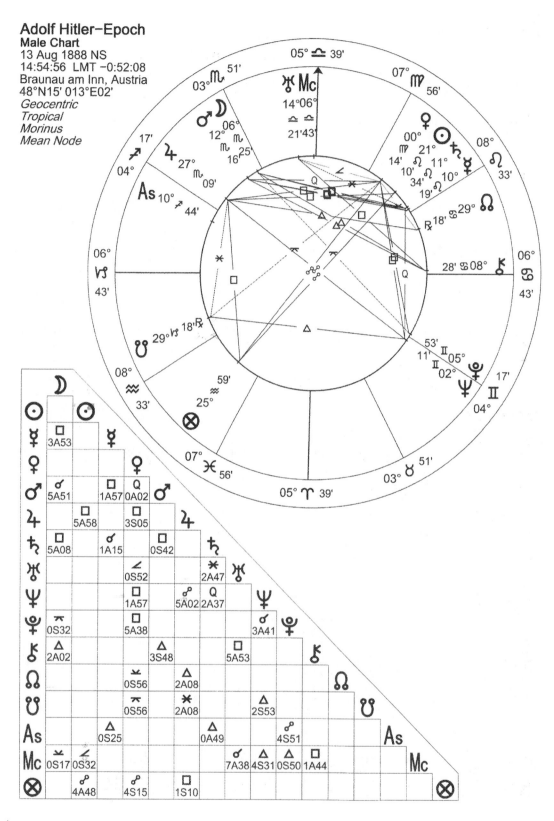

Adolf Hitler – Horoscopes

Adolf Hitler was born on the 20th April, 1889 at half past six in the evening at Braunau-am-Inn, Austria. His Epoch* occurred on the 13th August, 1888, at five to three in the afternoon. Examination of his Epoch chart and aspect grid (see Figure 3) shows that Neptune conjoint Pluto in Gemini in the 6th House leads a bowl shaping. This indicates that Hitler was an idealist who advocated a cause, or the furtherance of a mission. He was driven to seek and capture the other half of experience that he felt he was lacking. The Neptune – Pluto conjunction forms a mutable T-square in opposition to Jupiter in Scorpio in the 12th House both of which are square to Venus at the focal point at the short arm of the T in Virgo in the 9th House. This implies that he tried to adjust to intangible difficulties within his fondness for study, intelligent interests and travel but not without nervous strain. The Sun in Leo – Moon in Scorpio polarity gave him a determined, austere, hard yet ardent and even sensual nature; his internal nature was quite hidden beneath the hard exterior. The 8th – 11th House polarity indicates the delay he met in getting his career underway because of indecision about progress achieved against effort spent on any chosen career. The Moon trine Chiron suggests that he found helpful, protective support from others within societies and groups. His Morin Point in the 1st Capricorn decanate shows that he was a persistent, shrewd, self-controlled personality achieving success through hard work. Saturn (the ruler) lies in Leo in the 8th House conjoint Mercury and square Mars, showing that his

- -

*Notice that, at birth, the Moon is below the Earth (Morin Point) and is decreasing in light so that his Epoch will be 4th Order. The position of the Morin Point is male and that of the Moon is negative (neutral). Only an irregular, 3rd variation Epoch is valid for a male birth.

Figure 4: Birth Chart and Aspect Grid for Adolf Hitler.

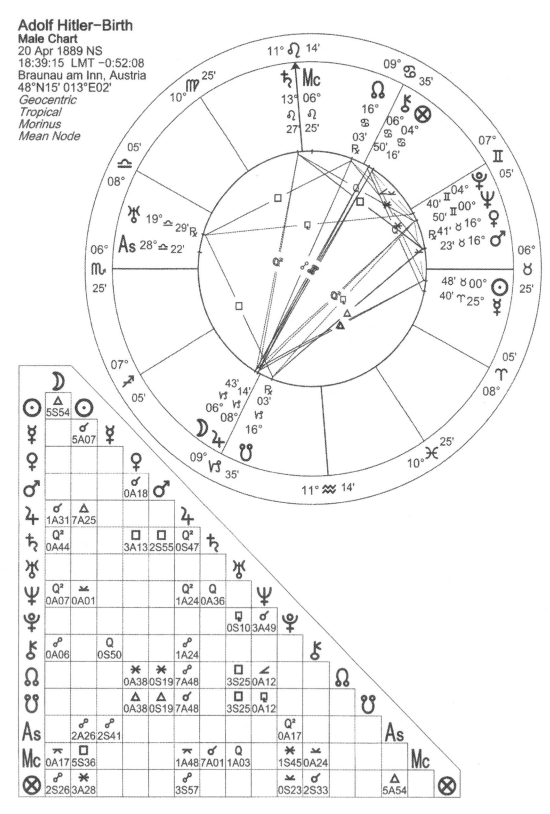

enjoyment of life did not come easily to him. He would have had an energetically strained mind without width but with great power of concentration and drive. His results would have had to be battled for (struggle?).

This Epoch generates an Ideal Birth time of twenty to seven in the - evening of the 20th April, 1889. Examination of the Birth chart (see Figure 4) reveals a West emphasis indicating that Hitler's destiny lay in others' hands and/or under prevailing conditions. The South emphasis shows objectivity rather than subjectivity. Overall there is a splay-type shaping indicating a highly individual person, who robustly resists pigeon-holing. There is a sharp, quintile-family kite with the Moon conjoint Jupiter in Capricorn in the 3rd House as its focal point. Chiron in Cancer in the 9th House is exactly opposite the Moon and is bi-decile to Saturn in Leo in the 10th House and to Neptune conjoint Pluto (the ruler) in Gemini in the 8th House. The strain imparted to the personality from this particular kite can hardly be excessive but may well have stimulated his mentality. At the least the kite does link all these planets together. The Sun in Taurus – Moon in Capricorn polarity shows a practical, careful, independent and vital person and the 7th - 3rd Houses polarity shows that he enjoyed being involved in the mainstream of human activity. The Sun is exactly semisextile to Neptune and confirms an attraction for music and art. The Moon conjoint Jupiter shows optimism, good health and a lucky journey through life; it is biquintile to Neptune revealing good sensitivity and is opposite to Chiron, which emphasises his need to make good contacts with informed people, whom he admires. Retrograde Venus, exalted in Taurus in exact conjunction with Mars in the 7th House both square to Saturn, reveals to us the source of all his troubles with the opposite sex. His Morin Point in Scorpio shows the potentially criminal side of his nature but also how he could achieve success by means of a thrusting, purposeful nature with a capacity for hard work. Pluto (the ruler) in

Gemini in the 8th House gave him his obsession with mobility (both practically and in the abstract as in "mobilisation of the masses") and his compelling need for overall comprehension (resulting in his utter conviction that he was right). It indicates also that his death would have been in a public place under unfortunate circumstances.

Notice that, for both Epoch and Birth charts, the Neptune – Pluto conjunction assumes considerable personal importance for Hitler as indicated.

Because astrologers previously have had difficulty reconciling Hitler's character with the more favourable interpretations of his Birth chart alone that is based on the traditional Ascendant in Libra, we shall now see that the combined interpretation (see Appendices 2a and 2b for the separate interpretations), based on his Scorpio Morin Point at Birth, coupled with the Sun in Leo – Moon in Scorpio polarity at his Epoch, describes him much more closely.

Minimised Person Summary with Biographical Extracts

Character

General: *Hitler was austere with an inclination to be rather hard. He had a very fixed and determined nature with practical abilities, a shrewd mind, ambition and inner stability.* 'His single-mindedness, inflexibility, ruthlessness in discarding all hindrances and cynical adroitness, all-or-nothing gambler's instinct for the highest stakes and demagoguery, all came together in one over-riding element in Hitler's drive: his boundless egomania. The use of propaganda to mobilise the masses and achieve power became his aphrodisiac.' Being highly individual with a robust resistance to pigeon-holing, very independent and strong-willed *he could, at times, be proud, arrogant and too positive.* 'Putsi Hanfstaengl said "Rather there are a number of images, all called Adolf Hitler that can only, with difficulty, be brought together in overall relation to each other."' At his worst he showed a criminal personality that sought fulfilment of personal aims without regard for the feelings of others. 'He was hypersensitive to personal criticism, having an inability to engage in rational argument with rapid resort to extraordinary outbursts of uncontrolled temper. All the histrionics of the Prima Donna and his aversion to any institutional anchoring were factors of an unbalanced personality repeatedly throughout his life.' *His internal nature was quite hidden underneath his hard exterior* yet he did have optimism and a love of show. 'Hitler, the playful youngster, became idle, resentful, rebellious, sullen, stubborn and purposeless with a lack of discipline for any systematic work. However, he would always bounce back, dressing to match the occasion, preoccupied with impact and impression and carefully avoiding anything potentially embarrassing or inviting ridicule.' *Additionally he was strongly influenced by his senses, whether they were passionate, emotional or mental.*

Mentality: Hitler's aptitude for making very carefully thought-out plans and schemes generally meant that they were carried out successfully. These were chiefly concerned with conventional ideals relating to physical objects and to personal surroundings. His mind was retentive so that he rarely forgot anything he learned but his emotional bias sometimes made it difficult for him to separate fact from fiction. On the other hand his great sensitivity enabled him to read character well. 'Hitler had a quick mind, formidable memory and biting wit.'

He tended to allow his critical faculty too much of his thought so that, coupled with a constant fuss about detail, it interfered with the harmony of his life and distressed his personality. His ability to express himself in creative, happy ways became limited so that his enjoyment of his life did not come easily. His mental and nervous power was basically limited resulting in dullness but his particular energetically strained mind gave him great power of concentration and drive, although still lacking width. There was a patient working out of what he began but not with ease. His results had to be battled for (Struggle – "Mein Kampf"). *The narrowness engendered and the difficulty endured produced selfishness and egocentricity. Accordingly sternness was given. Although he was fond of study* (he read many, many books), *of intellectual interests* (Art, Architecture, Biogenetics, Politics) *and of travel, he tended to become disappointed in these.* His spiritual energy together with his stimulated sensation seeking and his compelling need to achieve comprehension produced inventiveness but also impetuosity, eccentricity and fanaticism.

Lifestyle: He was naturally inquisitive about his immediate surroundings and family. *As an idealist engaged in a vital, but introspective search for the meaning of life, he advocated some cause or furtherance of a mission* (His cause was the National Socialism of the German masses as the means of saving Germany and converting it into a world power through fascism). *However, thoughts of death and of the after-life only developed when he was older. As a persistent, controlled personality with an obsession about mobility he achieved success through hard work.* 'Hitler mobilised the masses with his stirring speeches travelling by aeroplane (the first politician to do this) from one venue to the next.' *He had self-containment partly because he was set-off against a half of experience from which he was excluded so that his tendency was to go out and capture it.* 'Hitler left home at sixteen to live in Vienna.'   There were personal emphases in his life (he was Austrian but yearned to be German; he wanted to be an artist and then an architect; he volunteered to serve in WW1 and then recognised his own ability as a demagogue immediately after, which led him to pursue a rapidly developing, keen interest in propaganda and politics) in which his particular, yet impersonal temperament jutted out into experience according to his own, very special, tastes. He was an intense person who could not be limited to any steady point of application. 'He refused to seek promotion in the army and refused chairmanships because this would lead to too much organisational and administrative work.' His awkward certainty to every approach he took to the problems of life *made it difficult for him when he was not in a position to lead.* 'Hitler had to be sole leader of the Nazi party.' *However, he expressed the resulting disruptiveness with its ensuing paradoxical results through charming, harmonious yet eccentric ways.*

He was attracted to music, art, dancing and cautiously to psychism and the mystical. 'Hitler was a fanatical admirer of Wagner and was captivated by the grandeur of the buildings of Vienna and Munich. He encountered "Ostrava" magazine of the occult in Vienna.' He also tended towards day-dreaming (grandiose fantasy), philanthropy, retirement (he enjoyed his own company and Berchtesgaden) and matters of the sea.

Relationships

<u>People:</u> *He had something to give to his fellows either constructively* (his opinions) *or vindictively* (revenge for perceived slights). His ability to succeed here was enhanced by the ease with which he got involved with people. People sought his advice on important matters because he had such good insight. He enjoyed being in the mainstream of human activity and he had a talent for getting people to support him in his enterprises. Generally he was eager to reciprocate when others needed his help, which benefitted him in his long-range goals. *In turn he found helpful, protective support from others within societies and groups.* 'Dieter Eckhart, among others, became his mentor during his early years with the Nazi party.' With his easy-going personality he needed to be more aggressive in making beneficial, personal contacts especially with informed people (like the Hanfstaengls). In the same vein he encouraged contacts with people whom he admired 'such as Drexler, Ludendorff and Lueger' since they stimulated his development. He knew how to use opportunities that came through others, sometimes exceeding the rewards enjoyed by those who made the opportunities available.

Highly sensitive to his external environment he experienced the unbalanced parts of himself through the ways in which others saw him. Accordingly, he was never quite sure that he was seen as proper in their eyes. Thus he became defensive when others showed an interest in him because he questioned their motives. He was unsure whether their interest was physical or intellectual. *He had met responsibility through the affairs of others either through financial worries or through losses caused by them. He therefore tried to avoid being obligated to others although his circumstances indicated that he could not really escape it. He compared his resources with those of others as though he thought his self-worth was to be determined solely by his personal and material assets.* 'He became a very rich man as a result of the sales of "Mein Kampf"'.' Despite all this he needed to try to give people a chance to show their intentions before he jumped to conclusions.

Friends: He always seemed to make concessions when a situation developed that caused disharmony between himself with near others. His conciliatory manner endeared him to those with whom he was in close personal contact. 'This behaviour became particularly noticeable in the Berlin bunker at the end of WW2.' Outside of his interest in politics Hitler's life was largely a void but he was also highly secretive about anything at all connected with his private life. As a teenager he became close to August Kubicek with whom he shared a love of music, especially the opera. He developed little feeling for humans partly due to his WW1 experiences but formed good relationships with his dogs. He became distraught during WW1 when his dog, Foxl, could not be found.'

Family: Hitler experienced unfortunate separation from, and the death of his mother. He also experienced the death of two of his loved ones. 'He loved his mother but received no affection from his father. He may have witnessed his father beating his mother and he became closely attached to her. He provided her with indefatigable care while she was dying with cancer and became prostrate with grief.'

Partner: Hitler had a strong and robust ability to enjoy sexual life and all things of beauty but not with delicacy. *He was ardent and serious about sexual affairs but also sensual, if not somewhat perverted, that made him go to excess in love.* Shy earlier (he admired Stephanie of Linz from a distance), he wanted others to bring him out and he tried to draw

others to him quietly but finally the world passed him by.   He
developed unreasonable expectations of the opposite sex owing to
powerful self-delusions he had been holding for many years. Silently
he collected one chip on his shoulder after another, after another. . . . .
*He tended to adjust to, or to by-pass, or to put up with difficulties due to a lack
of partnership but not without nervous strain.* 'Kubicek's view was that
Hitler was out rightly misogynist. His celibate, no meat, no alcohol and
no dealings with women life-style justified his ideological morals but
acutely disturbed and repressed his sexual development.

He might have married for financial gain or simply because he
didn't like living alone, which would not have been the best reasons. It
would have been better to marry because he felt he had met his ideal
mate. Possibly he could have found a permanent relationship early in
his life. 'However, Hitler came to regard women only as an adornment
in a man's world. The inconsequential and feather-brained Eva Braun,
and perhaps Mimi Reiter, suited the type of relaxation and repose that
Hitler sought but Geli Raubal had affected him emotionally. She
committed   suicide,   primarily   because   of   his   overbearing
possessiveness, whereupon Hitler became hysterical and fell into a
deep depression.' *If he and his partner had complimented each other* and
were equally fascinated by change and progress they would have been
very happy and mutually supportive. *He worked very hard to convince
his partner, Eva, that he cared when probably it wasn't necessary. She already
gave him all the support he needed to exploit his later career.*

Career

Early: When criminal tendencies were resisted honest success was
achieved by means of a thrusting, purposeful nature and a capacity for
hard work. *Although misfortune and obstacles beset his path* he
nevertheless had a strong tendency to a lucky journey through life.
Overall his fate was in the hands of others (e.g. Captain Mayr of the
Reichswehr, Drexler and Eckhart of the Nazi party and Röhm of the SA

developed and promoted his interests) and/or depended on his surrounding circumstances (the parlous condition of Germany before, during and following WW1). *He was delayed getting his career underway probably because he couldn't decide which field would give him the greatest return for his efforts.* A routine job was not for him because it would have denied him the full development of his creative potential. 'He refused promotion into routine, administrative jobs.' *Only a career with a future interested him.* 'He found he was a propagandist, demagogic politician par excellence.' A job that allowed him self-determination (as it did!) gave him a say about his growth and progress in his field. *There were indeed many opportunities for applying his skills (at the time) where they were most needed. However, initially, he was deeply occupied with finding a job that would give him security in his later years* (such as a great artist or architect) *rather than one that would permit him to exploit his creativity as fully as possible. He was able to back off a little and re-examine his motivations (during the four years of WW1). He then discovered that his potential ("I can speak") could satisfy certain needs of the larger society. When he focussed on providing a service that made demands on his talent, security for the future became a natural by-product. He was best suited,* and especially adapted, *for working with the public, which allowed him to expand his range of influence as his skills improved* (speaker -> drummer -> Nazi party leader -> Fuhrer of Germany). Giving the public advice was the career that required the kind of talents that he had. It made a good choice for him. *Communications, government service, politics, social service and vocational guidance were some of the ways he could and did use his talents to make a worthwhile contribution to society.* Additionally journalism (he wrote many articles for the "Volkish Beobachter" party newspaper), writing (author of "Mein Kampf"), broadcasting (he gave innumerable speeches), law (he made a point of making progress legally after his failed, illegal putsch) or any of the communications media, would have been appropriate for his talents and temperament.

Middle: He underestimated his ability to make an important contribution to society (it took a long time for him to accept that he could become Germany's leader). He was extremely sensitive to human frailty and knew how to solve the problems it causes. His sensitivity to unacceptable social conditions forced him to make sacrifices to ensure their elimination (the Jews and the Marxists). Many legal resources were available to help him force the public to re-examine the social values involved. *He also knew how important it was to plan for the future so that he could easily find a way to make the kind of investment that would assure him of some financial independence in his later years. However, frustration caused by meeting closed outlets, caused poor organisation and resentment at being kept down.* 'Hitler was rejected earlier by the Vienna Art Academy and later Hindenburg refused to offer him the Chancellorship of Germany in 1932 when he was the leader of the most elected party.' He was greatly concerned about monetary resources but because he rarely looked back his future rewards were limited only by the commitment he was willing to make to them. *He showed a careful interest in psychic matters.* 'During the late 1930s and WW2 he received astrological predictions from Kraft.' *He would have made a good magnetic healer.*

Late: He had the ability to deal with big schemes involving the organisation and carrying out of huge plans. *As a splendid leader in the affairs of the world he had the vision and the readiness to change old ways. Nothing was as satisfying to him as knowing that he had helped to make the world a better place for everyone (particularly German).*

Health

He had good health, vitality, physical strength, endurance and the prospect of a long life. *Depression may have been frequent.* 'Hitler had the capacity to channel disappointment and depression into outright aggression.' *He needed to guard against excesses in love that could have injured or diseased his heart. There was danger of accidents by burns, scalds and falling. Physical overstrain was risked.* His death occurred in a public place (the Berlin bunker) under unfortunate, tragic circumstances (he married Eva Braun, whereupon they both committed suicide within two days).

<u>Reference:</u> "Hitler: 1889 – 1936, Hubris", I. Kershaw, W. W. Norton, New York, USA, 1999.

- -

CHAPTER 8
Josef Stalin

"One death is a tragedy, a million deaths is a statistic"

Josef Stalin was the General Secretary of the Soviet Union's Central Committee from 1922 until his death in 1953. He launched a command economy of rapid, drastic industrialisation supported by genocidal, agricultural collectivisation. In the late 1930's he ruthlessly conducted "The Great Purge" (Terror) of Soviet society. In 1941 the Soviet Union joined the Allies to play the major part  in the defeat of Nazi Germany in World War II. Subsequently he installed communist governments in Eastern Europe forming the "Iron Curtain" and creating the "Cold War". He undertook efforts to improve his public image and under his leadership education, medical care and equal opportunity for all were initiated throughout the Soviet Union.

Josef Stalin – Horoscopes

Stalin was born on the 18th December, 1878 at 03:01[8], to Beso and

- -

*The Moon lay above the Earth (Morin Point) and was decreasing in light so that the Order of his Epoch was 2nd. The position of the Moon is negative (neutral) and that of the Morin Point is male. Thus his Epoch will be irregular 2nd or 3rd variation; the former fitting him significantly better.

Figure 5: Epoch Chart and Aspect Grid for Josef Stalin.

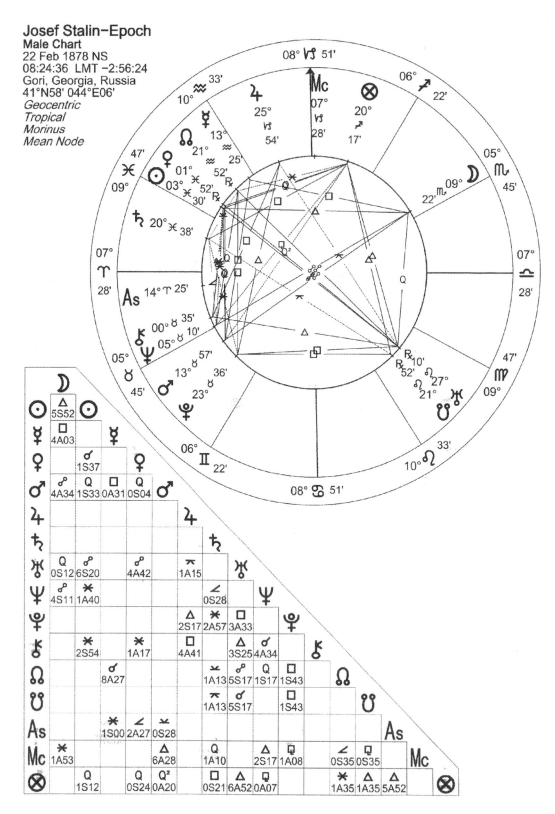

Josef Stalin–Epoch
Male Chart
22 Feb 1878 NS
08:24:36 LMT −2:56:24
Gori, Georgia, Russia
41°N58' 044°E06'
Geocentric
Tropical
Morinus
Mean Node

Keke, in Gori (a town plagued by gang warfare), Georgia, Russia. His Epoch* occurred on the 22nd February, 1878 at 08:25. Examination of his Epoch chart and aspect grid (see figure 5) shows a bucket shaping with Mars opposite the Moon as the rim and Uranus in Leo in the 6th House as the somewhat anticlockwise handle planet. This means that Stalin had a particular and uncompromising direction to his life-effort (as an ambitious Bolshevik-Marxist). The Uranus handle shows conservative eccentricity and a desire for freedom with clever use of inventive ideas to aid his work in a need to be involved in activities that would show how valuable he was to others. The strong, fixed T-square having Mercury at the focal, short arm of the T shows that he let difficulties remain and put up with them, causing stress, but that his aim was to get together with others for a common purpose. The Sun in Pisces-Moon in Scorpio polarity made him seem too hard and selfish but showed that his inner nature was more kindly. The Sun in the 12th House-Moon in the 8th House polarity reveals his insight into people's motivations and his poise when under pressure. **The Sun conjoint Venus** indicates artistic capability while the Moon quintile Uranus shows his desire for the unusual, particularly at home. His Morin Point in the 1st Aries decanate accounts for his frank, free-handed disposition and the ruler, Mars in Taurus in the 2nd House reveals his obstinately forceful nature and his energetic interest in both finance and agriculture. The Epoch chart shown in Figure 5 generates the Birth chart and aspect grid for Stalin as shown in Figure 6. Examination of this chart shows that Uranus in Virgo in the 11th House leads an overall locomotive-shaping, meaning that Stalin had a need for a problem to be solved in the social and intellectual world around him to justify his drive towards power. He was moved more by external factors than from within himself. Uranus forms a Grand Trine in Earth with **the Sun conjoint Venus** at the end of Sagittarius in the 3rd

Figure 6: Birth Chart and Aspect Grid for Josef Stalin

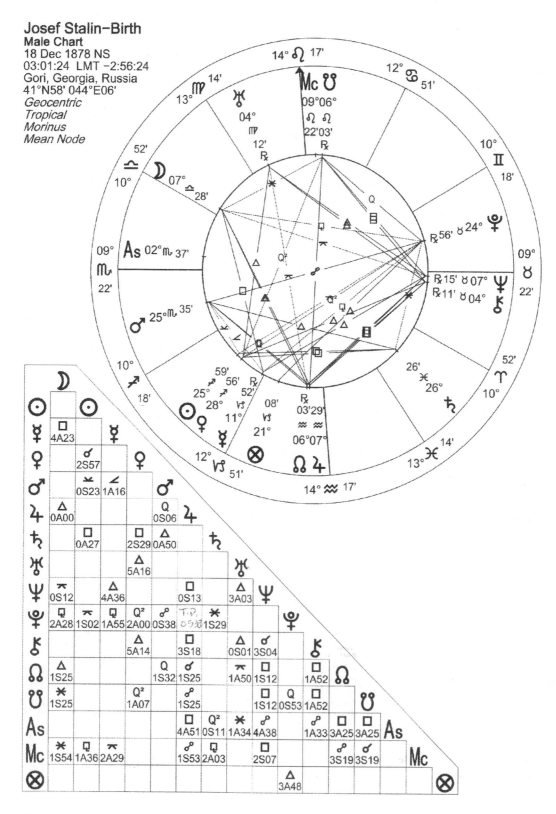

House and with Chiron conjoint Neptune in Taurus in the 7th House. Peculiar conditions in marriage/partnership are indicated with a hidden arrangement about these. His partners were likely to have been spiritually minded or artistic. Pluto (the ruler) that is opposition to Mars and sesquiquadrate to both the Moon in Libra in the 12th House and to retrograde Mercury in Capricorn in the 3rd House, lies at the focal point of a sesquiquadrate kite. This imparts considerable strain to his character and emphasises his obsession with wealth, his need to achieve permanence, his vital search for the meaning of life and his great concern over resources. **The Sun conjoint Venus** is square Saturn in Pisces in the 6th House, which in turn is trine Mars in Scorpio in the 2nd House and sextile Pluto (the ruler) in Taurus in the 8th House. This shows that Stalin's artistic self-expression was hurtfully limited to his disadvantage and that his life was hard, leading him towards self-pity. He achieved much but his tendency was to overstrain making him pugnacious, bad-tempered and explosive. He experienced envy in his professional life. However, the Moon is exactly trine Jupiter in Aquarius in the 4th House. Stalin, despite all, was optimistic with a strong tendency to a lucky journey through life meeting good opportunities and helpful people but he realised that he had to stand on his own. The Moon is also exactly quincunx Neptune. This provided him with good sensitivity that encouraged people to seek his help. The Morin Point in Scorpio shows the criminal side of his personality but also his capacity for deserved success by means of his thrusting, purposeful nature and a capacity for hard work. Retrograde Mercury in Capricorn in the 3rd House, semisquare Mars and square to the Moon, shows his highly active, analytical mentality resulting in a deep and weighty thinker. All told, every planet in Stalin's Birth chart is important for one reason or another. Stalin was always different and exceptional. Even his youth was dramatic and adventurous. His Person Summary, derived by combining the interpretations of his Epoch and Birth charts, together with biographical abstracts within brackets or apostrophes, provides a brief, particular and composite description of him.

Person Summary and Biographical Extracts

Character

General: 'Stalin was proud to consider himself a practical hard man.' This fits well with a nature that seemed too hard, obstinately forceful, conventional, unyielding, jealous and selfish. However, his inner nature was, in fact, more kindly and sympathetic than it seemed outwardly. His self-expression was through his affections, through beauty, art and gentle ways with even a touch of effeminacy but most of this was strongly held in check, causing self-pity (he blamed himself for the deaths of his two wives becoming emotionally distraught – so also died his last warm feelings for humanity, whereupon he devoted himself to Bolshevism) and a galvanic, tense, emotional response that gave a smouldering temper about to break out. Any subsequent explosion would end conditions at once and strongly force new beginnings but with unhappy results. His frank, open, outspoken and free-handed disposition sat well with his independent behaviour. Robust, courageous, overactive and over-quick, his fairly strong personality contained ambition and endurance. 'All these characteristics were shown plentifully throughout his youth.' His good, harmonious side revealed sincerity, sensitivity and hopefulness but later his outlook became utilitarian. He developed an obsession with wealth (eventually he owned several dachas) and felt compelled to achieve permanence (to this end he wrote high quality "position" articles based on Bolshevik- Marxism). 'Later, many statues were erected to honour him.'

<u>Mentality:</u> Stalin had quick and accurate perception added to great powers of comparison and imagination. His communication was expressed in all ways in which there may be a getting-together with others for a common purpose or objective (at an early age he joined a socialist workers party). Friends so made were mental rather than emotional companions. His mind turned to mental interests of a scientific kind and to those deemed to be for the good of humanity, but also towards a linking with other minds similarly motivated (he "devoured" Lenin's newspaper "Iskri").

Highly active, pensive and analytical mentally, he became a very deep and weighty thinker. His greatest strength was absorbing knowledge for use in developing future plans. However, his depth could prevent him from communicating smoothly when trying to express what he knew. He would become bogged down trying to find the right word to say all that he wanted to, precisely. 'Consequently all Stalin's sentences became sharp and crisp statements.' Thus his greatest difficulty lay in public relations because others would lose patience with all that he was trying to construct mentally. However, he became more easily understood later in life.

He was insatiably curious and eager to know as much as possible about a variety of subjects. 'He "ate" books.' However, he was easily distracted so that his attention started to wander. Fortunately his day-dreaming was brought to good fulfilment because he considered imagination and psychism in a practical yet aesthetic way. As a result he developed a large fund of ideas but imagined that he would never get the chance to use them.

He had refinement, one of his girlfriends, Pelagaya, attested to his good taste; some artistic genius (while still a teenager he had several poems published and musicality - as a boy he became a trained alto soloist. 'He had good rhythm. Later, he loved singing Georgian songs and declaiming poetry.'

<u>Lifestyle:</u> Stalin had the capacity to enjoy life in all its dimensions. He dug deeply into life and poured forth the result of his gathered experiences with unremitting zeal. He was fond of intellectual pursuits, of acquiring knowledge, of debate and argument and was always at the front. He contended aggressively for rights and privileges and showed considerable resource for regaining any lost prestige. He often said more than he meant to because he was enthusiastic, energetic, enterprising, progressive and aspiring. He was ambitious and did not miss many opportunities, either by being thwarted by obstacles or by failure. At his worst he had a criminal personality (early on he supported Bolshevism by robbery, extortion, etc.) seeking fulfilment of personal aims without regard for the feelings of others (he neglected both his wives). Initially he seemed to do things the hard way but that helped him to achieve later on (he became the sole practically experienced member of the Central Committee). During this early time he may have gone through paranoid periods during which he got bogged down in his own depth but he was more than able to plod his own way back out. His desire for fulfilment was hampered by the necessity to make some adjustment to his habits (slowly he transformed himself from brigand to Head of State) and by letting difficulties remain (such as trouble with government spies) and putting up with them but not without nervous strain. His desire was for the unusual and unconventional, especially in the home (he loved views of nature and tending his lemon trees). This eccentricity was apt to run away with itself and his desire for freedom became too arrogant but splendid leadership was shown when he was in the right place for it, e.g. as Head of State.

He had tendencies to want to retire (to his dachas) and to philanthropy (he gave donations to old friends out of built-up savings from his salary).

Relationships

<u>People:</u> Initially Stalin assumed that everyone was superior to him and that he owed them his service. There is a degree of masochism here that may have caused him to rationalise the fact that others took advantage of him. He was easily affected by the behaviour of others because it would have given them an advantage over him (he overreacted vindictively to avenge slights). The rapport he had with people made them feel comfortable and confident that he would be able to help them. His permissiveness in relationships was such that it gave him the mobility he needed to prove himself before the public. However, he had to be alert to the possibility of professional envy from his fellow workers (mostly from Beria, the chief of the Secret Service) and to be discriminating about the people with whom he shared information. There was the possibility of treachery; for example, his spy detecting abilities failed him (and several others) in the case of Malinovsky, leading to the arrest, imprisonment and exile of senior Bolshevik leaders, including Stalin. Later, the world (i.e. the West) was inclined to misjudge him.

<u>Friends:</u> Popular, Stalin attracted friends and was quick to make acquaintances of good social standing. For example, they showed him congeniality, welcomed him into their company and from among whom he would marry. 'Both his wives, Kato and Nadya, were socially superior to him.'

<u>Family:</u>   Although mostly held severely in check Stalin's self-expression was through his affections, through beauty, art and gentle ways.

<u>Partner:</u> Stalin's ability to love and enjoy sexual life and all things of beauty was strengthened and made more robust but less delicate. He committed some acts of indiscretion (probably this was the reason that he had to leave school just before he was due to complete it). His partners would likely have been spiritually-minded (they

embraced Bolshevism and ideally with his 2nd wife, Nadya, because she shared his need to exploit his potential) or artistic. He might well have had problems in relationships because he attracted people who made excessive demands (e.g. Nadya) and expected him to comply with them. A disappointing childhood may have conditioned Stalin to escape into marriage, which was hardly the best reason for such a demanding relationship. Possibly he chose someone (Kato), who was as insecure as he was, out of sentimental pity. Such an early marriage was unrealistic because he needed to gain greater perspective about what he wanted to accomplish in life. 'His neglect of Kato for his career led to her death and "destroyed his ability to love".' Having children too soon was burdensome (he left his child with his in-laws) because he hadn't clearly defined his goals. 'In fact, throughout his life, he abandoned many of his children for his career. Yet he had good relations with youngsters.' It would have been ideal if he and his partner had shared similar objectives. However, there were strange, or peculiar, conditions in marriage (he tormented Nadya by playing upon her nature, which may have contributed to her committing suicide) or partnerships, or a hidden arrangement about them.

Career

Early: Stalin's childhood circumstances gave him the opportunity to develop without psychological problems so that as he matured he was able to integrate the various forces within him. His ability to succeed was strengthened by his basically harmonic nature, which enabled him to handle conflict or frustration before it became a major crisis. He may have had to maintain a low profile in his achievements. He had a strong tendency to a lucky journey through life, during which he met good opportunities and helpful people. 'He himself was amazed by the help he received from complete strangers.'   His life, based on unusual objectives (he combined education and art with violence to pursue Bolshevik Marxist Ideology) was never uninteresting. His fate was precipitated by his impulsive and headstrong tendencies as well as by his fearless, pioneering and progressive spirit. His destiny was in his own hands but there would be misfortune in his life (e.g. his father left when he was 4 resulting in a rough upbringing in childhood). He pursued a vital search for the meaning of life (he developed a low opinion of the value of human life). He was moved by external factors rather than from those within himself and so had a need for a problem to be solved in the social and intellectual world around him. Thus he became ready to join societies for good "-isms" (e.g. Bolshevism and Marxism). There was compulsion to achieve here, but not without trouble. Treachery, foolishness and obsession with "-isms" could well have ensued. However, if his criminal tendencies could have been resisted, honest success could have been achieved by means of a thrusting, purposeful nature and a capacity for hard work. At this stage he had not realised that anything he wanted to achieve carried with it the responsibility for learning new skills. Converting his potential into skills probably required considerable sacrifice. However, he worked hard to develop them because he knew he could make a good living by applying them in his chosen field. He had incredible insight into what motivates people in their behaviour and was gifted at handling them and their problems. It could have been painful to know so much about people for it suggested that he had an obligation to use his creativity to help others. Making a contribution that improved the quality of life for the public would have allowed him to reach the limits of his potential. Thus he became qualified for a career in a professional capacity that required him to help others solve their problems effectively. Some outlets for his talent included financial and/or psychological counselling, social work or medicine. Or he could have preferred writing, illustration or design (Stalin enjoyed writing letters and even edited "Pravda"). His energetic, practical and executive business ability was expressed in financial ways and also in work for the growing things of the earth (i.e. for agriculture).

His early conditioning stimulated him to make the most of any situation, for which he should have been grateful to his parents. He was very aware that he would have to stand on his own but was easily distracted from this because he felt obliged to go along with his parents' views about what he should do with his life. 'His cobbler father wanted him to become a cobbler whereas his mother wanted him to become a priest.' He wanted, and should have chosen, a career that allowed him to use his creativity, as a professional service, in helping people manage their material resources.

Middle: Stalin may have found himself in a job that did not accord with his true nature but he would have been unable to change it, and similarly with his habits and customs. There was a particular and uncompromising direction to his life-effort (Bolshevik Marxism) and he adapted his allegiances to lines along which he could make his efforts count for the most (he gave his support to Lenin throughout). He was aware that he had to stand on his own, having little concern for end-results, for preserving himself or for conserving his resources. Stalin considered his value important only to the larger purpose of helping people to improve their circumstances. By applying his talent he became an invaluable help to those who needed his aid and his competence. He would have become increasingly dissatisfied with himself unless he had become involved in activities that proved how valuable he was to others. It troubled him when he couldn't satisfy other people's needs and he never felt comfortable unless he had been helpful. He was pleased when he could show people how to become more self-sufficient by using their own resources effectively. People sought his help when they needed direction in their affairs. He could offer services that the public required and it would have appreciated his help in showing it how to become more successful (e.g. in education and in health).

Stalin placed a high premium on his services because he knew how valuable he was, knew how to capitalise on other people's needs and worked hard to provide them with the services they needed. He expected to be well paid and he enjoyed deservedly high earnings from his career. He satisfied his need for creative expression by using his skills in effective communication. His wealth of ideas was not enough to generate success. He had to be willing to promote them. Once his mind was made up he made every possible contact to put his plans into action. He had clever and inventive ideas to aid his work that involved frequent changes. For example, new ideas were applied to food and to precautions about health.

The most troublesome problem in his life, and a source of great concern, was finding the necessary financial resources to launch his plans (he took from agriculture and gave it to industrial development) but any financial advantage he gained helped him to achieve a more abundant life.

At some time, travelling, especially by sea (his early fund raising activities for Bolshevism included a period of piracy) was likely.

Late: Stalin mustn't have been afraid to invest heavily in his ability to rise above petty issues and reveal the enormous power of the values he had acquired. 'He collectivised agriculture and simultaneously instigated five-year industrialisation plans.' Although much was achieved his tendency was to overstrain through overdoing (particularly during World War II) making him pugnacious and bad-tempered. 'He was often abusive to colleagues.'

Health

Stalin had good health but overdoing impaired his vitality making him liable to minor accidents (two carriage incidents as a boy damaged his left arm and both his legs). He had a tendency to falls, chills and orthopaedic troubles (his right hand, which he kept hidden, was thinner than his left). Eccentricity occurred in faddy ways, especially over health troubles possibly involving his intestines, caused by worry and over-concern with matters of detail. His sleep tended to be heavy and there was danger from gas, drugs, poisons and anaesthetics. 'He could well have been poisoned by warfarin that exacerbated his cerebral haemorrhage at the time of his death. This occurred at a public dinner at his Kuntsevo residence.'

He had a powerful, but possibly somewhat discordant, voice.

References: a) "Young Stalin", Simon Sebag Montefiore, Phoenix, Orion Books, London, 2007.

b) "Stalin: The Court of the Red Tsar", Simon Sebag Montefiore, Phoenix, Orion Books, London, 2004.

c) The Internet, Wikipedia, Joseph Stalin, 2009.

- -

CHAPTER 9

Napoleon Bonaparte

"Who was the greatest general of his day?"
"In this age, in past ages, in any age: Napoleon"
Arthur Wellesley, Duke of Wellington.

Napoleon Bonaparte was a military and political leader of France whose actions shaped European politics in the early 19th century. Born in Corsica and trained as an artillery officer in mainland France Napoleon rose to prominence under the 1st French Republic and led successful campaigns against the 1st and 2nd Coalitions arrayed against France. In 1799 he staged a coup d'état and installed himself as 1st Consul. Five years later he crowned himself Emperor of the French. He turned the armies of the French Empire against every European power and dominated continental Europe through a series of military victories. He maintained France's sphere of influence by the formation of external alliances and the appointment of family members and friends to rule other European countries as French client states.

The French invasion of Russia in 1812 marked a turning point in Napoleon's fortunes. His Grande Armée was badly damaged and never recovered fully. In 1813 the 6th Coalition defeated his forces at Leipzig. In 1814 the Coalition invaded France, forced Napoleon's abdication and exiled him to the island of Elba. In 1815 he escaped and returned to power but was defeated at the Battle of Waterloo.

He spent his last six years on the island of St. Helena under British

71

Figure 7: Epoch Chart and Aspect Grid for Napoleon Bonaparte

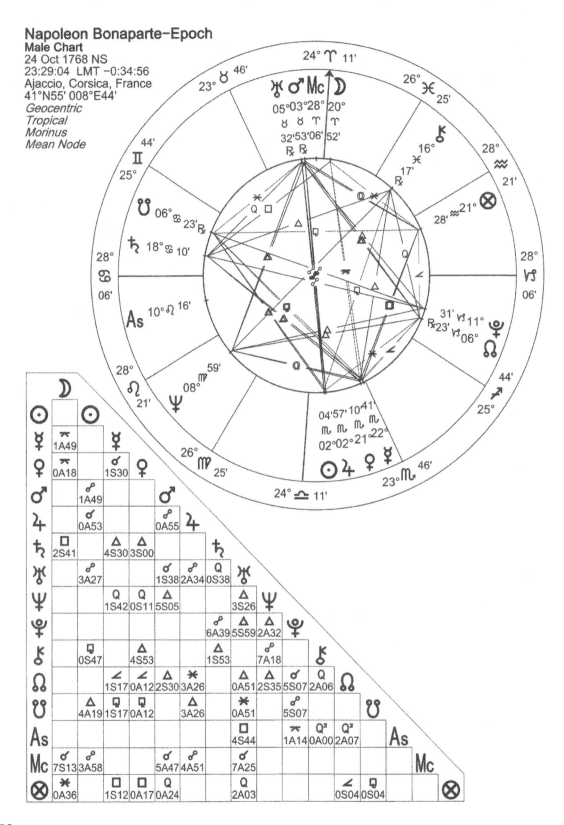

Napoleon Bonaparte–Epoch
Male Chart
24 Oct 1768 NS
23:29:04 LMT −0:34:56
Ajaccio, Corsica, France
41°N55' 008°E44'
Geocentric
Tropical
Morinus
Mean Node

supervision, dying there of stomach cancer. While he was considered a tyrant by his opponents, he is also remembered for establishing the Napoleonic Code, which laid the administrative and judicial foundation for much of Western Europe.

Napoleon Bonaparte – Horoscopes

Napoleon, the second son and child of Carlo and Letizia Bonaparte was born on the 15th August, 1769 at five to ten in the morning in Ajaccio, Corsica, France. His Epoch* occurred on the 24th October, 1768 at half past eleven at night. Examination of the Epoch chart and aspect grid (see Figure 7) reveals an overall See-Saw type shaping. This means that in one sense he had difficulty making his mind up and taking decisions but in another sense it also means that his decisions were thought out carefully. There is a Grand Trine in earth to the retrograde Mars – retrograde Uranus conjunction in Taurus in the 10th House that directly opposes the Sun – Jupiter conjunction in the first Scorpio decanate in the 4th House. Briefly, this indicates a strong practical, arrogant and passionate character, who is strongly attached to home and family, needing to make his-own way through favourable education and who finds difficulty in relationships with the opposite sex. A second Grand trine, this time in water, applies to the Mercury – Venus conjunction in the 3rd Scorpio decanate in the 5th House that includes Saturn rising in Cancer. This conjunction is quincunx the Moon (ruler) in Aries in the 10th House that is square to Saturn. All this suggests a struggle for

- -

*At birth the Moon is below the Earth and increasing in light meaning that his Epoch was 3rd Order. The sex of the positions of the Moon and of the Morin Point at birth were both female. Of the three possible sex Epochs available only the irregular, 3rd variation one can give rise to a male birth

Figure 8: Birth Chart and Aspect Grid for Napoleon Bonaparte.

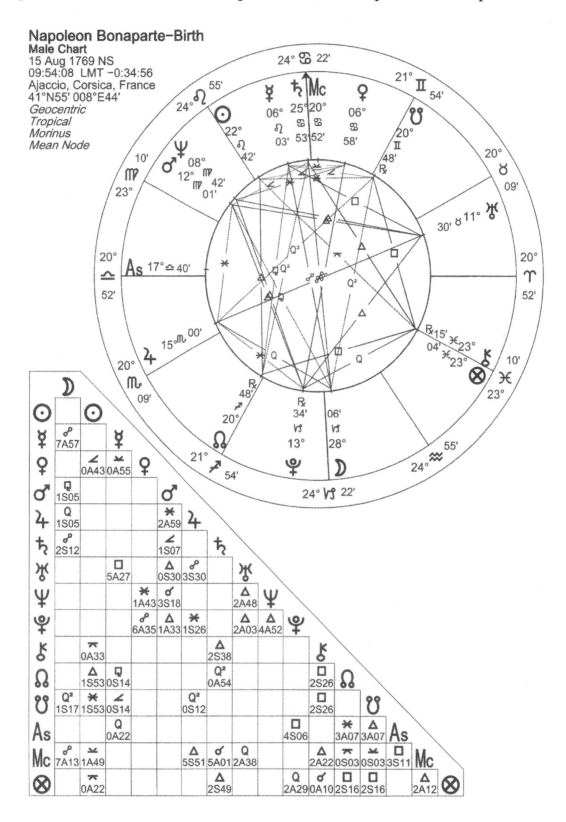

universal harmony, difficulties with women and his mother, a life lonely except for his chosen one and a tendency to meet hardships.

His Epoch chart generates his Ideal Birth chart and aspect grid (see Figure 8). Examination of this chart shows a Bucket shaping with Uranus as the somewhat conservative handle planet in Taurus in the 8th House (plus Chiron as a somewhat liberal handle in Pisces in the 6th House). Uranus is particularly emphasised in this chart, not only as a handle planet but also as the focal planet of a Grand-Trine-in-earth kite. This emphasises his galvanic force as an interest in science and the practical, particular direction of his life-effort (both military and political). Venus is the ruling planet (the Morin Point lies in Libra) in Cancer in the 9th House. This shows the charming side of his nature and his maternal-like care for loved ones. The following Person Summary provides us with his own, more detailed description:

Person Summary with Biographical Extracts

Character

General: Napoleon showed determined ambition coming from a strong character that was self-willed, assertive, insistent and positive. He had courage, resolution and independence. In relaxed mode he was cheerful and contented with his own ways and surroundings. His very strong passions resulted in very sharp likes and dislikes with a tendency to suddenness in his actions. Under stress he became pugnacious, bad-tempered, stubborn dogmatic, impulsive, jealous and even tyrannical. Now and then he was revolutionary, disruptive, awkward and brusque. Alternatively he could become overanxious, peevish, discontented, unhappy, obsessive and even hysterical. To outward appearance he could seem to be grasping, selfish and worldly externally but inside his heart pulled away from external things.

Mentality: Both his feelings and his intellect were well-developed. He was fond of study, intellectual interests and travel. He tended to be idealistic about his possessions and his spiritual ideas were calm and chaste yet he was liable to be critical about psychic matters. He had strange ideas about life, sex and death but these were mostly kept hidden. Although his mind was acute and would not wander he easily became restless, excitable and acrimonious, showing a lack of coolness, calmness and humility. 'Napoleon was talented, intelligent and passionate.'

Lifestyle: Napoleon's temperament was set on the conservative side, in which there was an element of the perennial child about him, who was unwilling to grow and transform the patterns of his youth. Thus he became a creature of habit, retaining many bad ones. He developed a hard interior nature containing exactitude and much practicality, coupled with a desire to put all new theories to the test. He liked to spend time alone but also needed to know that he was not left alone. He would check and re-check his actions to such an extent that he almost became a procrastinator. Then he would take the one action that he knew he was going to take all along. 'His success came not from luck but from an astute exploitation of opportunities that he saw before him.' Generally he tended to act at all times from a consideration of opposing views or through sensitiveness to contrasting and antagonistic possibilities. His restless personality was tempered by an easy-going and comfort-loving disposition. He showed a love of ground-breaking change that had to work against surrounding, inert resistance resulting in sudden outbreaks from within strained circumstances. His compulsive and magnetic leadership was either obeyed or violently broken. There are three quotations that would seem to be fitting for Napoleon: 1) "Blessed are the meek for they shall inherit the Earth." 2) "For the race is not always won by the swift, nor the battle by the strong."

3) "Don't take yourself too seriously; it makes it difficult for you to show any human weakness."
'He created a heroic image for public consumption that he was then obliged to live up to.'

Relationships

<u>Others:</u>   Sometimes Napoleon had difficulties with people who resented his lack of inhibitions.   Once he understood that not everyone could feel as liberated as he did, he could learn to cope with people who had to accept their frustrations.   However, generally, people were impressed with his ability to assert himself and they admired the way he defied any of society's rules that interfered with his desires.   He was able to do a great deal to help people become free of their inhibitions and hang-ups; he could teach them how to create a future of their own choosing, rather than remain confined to the past that only restricted them.   In fact it may have been difficult for him not to lose his own identity through helping others but he also realised that others' needs had a high priority and that his own personal desires had to come second.

<u>Friends:</u>   Napoleon had an amiable, hospitable and sympathetic personality that delighted in the company of friends and acquaintances.   'He became more confident in Auxonne, where he enjoyed his youth for the first time, becoming amenable to chatter.' Although he was basically friendly he was apprehensive about forming close relationships.   He could back away from advances but he also knew that he would be miserable if they did not exist.   On the other hand there were times when he put too much trust in others and was over friendly, which led to trouble when not restrained, e.g. after making Bernadotte King of Sweden, the latter then turned against him.

<u>Family:</u> His parents allowed him to express himself in his own way so that he assumed that everyone would allow him that privilege. 'He became morose, sombre and cantankerous at school in Brienne.' He was very attached to home and family but found it difficult to maintain an equal relationship with both parents. "His head told him one thing but his heart another." As he preferred his mother (he resented his father's obsequiousness) it made it difficult for him to establish his own identity. Fortuitously, he left home, aged nine, which gave him time to resolve this problem and so develop a better perspective. Probably, he was able to enjoy a favourable relationship with both parents while he could. He may well have decided that staying on his own was best for everyone concerned. The psychological realignment had to continue though since this attitude probably persisted in other, later relationships. However, his strong family ties meant that even after he had moved away from his birth place he returned often to renew old ties. 'He returned to Corsica three times in his middle to late teens.' His next main issue was coping with his responsibilities to family, which his parents considered his first priority. 'He looked after his family after his father's death.' It was probably with good reason that he rebelled since no-one else should determine his priorities for him. Overall, much depended on his ability to loosen the emotional ties to his family and to gravitate towards people he met socially.

Although it would have been difficult for him to manage to satisfy his responsibilities to his children he would still have had a career that satisfied his desire to achieve recognition for his services.

<u>Partner:</u> His affection was sympathetic, tender and somewhat maternal, or cherishing, in his desire to care for loved ones. He wanted to feel close to others but held himself back, creating inner tension instead, so that his desire for warmth and closeness became inhibited. The resulting sense of deprivation intensified his shyness and prevented easy response to what could have brought happiness.

This uneasy expression of affection meant that his relationships with women, and with his mother, were not easy.   This was his biggest problem because he wanted someone who could share everything with him. 'Josephine was Napoleon's first serious encounter with a mature woman.   He was lonely and became infatuated quickly but she was not the type to become devoted to her husband in the way that he wanted.'   He was uncomfortable as a lover and needed the support of the one he loved to make his achievements and successes seem meaningful and worthwhile.   'Josephine's unfaithfulness tended to destroy his will to succeed.'   The limitations on his affections though, had their reward in a serious one-pointed direction in that his life was lonely except for his chosen one. 'He loved Josephine through thick and thin.'   He had acquired good housekeeping ways but there was a lack of harmony in his home. He married a foreigner (Josephine was part Creole from Martinique) and Marie Louise, his second wife, was Austrian. He lived abroad after marriage (France, Italy, Egypt etc.) and he could have gone into such partnership for business or professional purposes.

Career

Early: Probably Napoleon had grown up in an austere environment (at school in Brienne). This increased his later determination to acquire as many comforts as possible. Education and training (thanks to his father) had increased his career options. It had become important for him to turn his talent into skills that allowed him to succeed later. 'He gained valuable political experience in Corsica as a youth.' As a result he was not so easily intimidated by those in authority. He created his life in terms of the past; from which most of his goals were based (he read the classics of an evening). He felt that barriers were holding him back (his Corsican background and his lack of wealth) but this was not the case. Initially he had to resolve some limitations (family ties) before he could feel comfortable in pursuing the kind of life that suited his identity. Also his sensitivity tended to slow his progress until he learnt to assert himself. However, others did not feel threatened because he was always considerate of their feelings. His first attempts to establish himself were filled with frustration (his teenage Corsican experiences disillusioned him) but he had to persist elsewhere (in France). He discovered that he had plenty of opportunities in life (he soon became Commander in Chief of the Army of Italy) and that "good luck" was to be expected (after the battle of Arcola). His galvanic force pointed to results of an outstanding nature in engineering and science (his excellent use of artillery; he joined the ideologues out of personal interest as well as for political gain). A career in politics, business, sales, public relations or working with children or young people would have suited his temperament. A prominent position, or responsible public post, was indicated.

Middle: There was a particularly uncompromising direction to his life-effort (towards power), showing little concern over end results, or to conserving his own physical resources (as a youth Napoleon always looked wan and unhealthy). He adapted his allegiances to lines along which he could make his efforts count for the most (e.g. his Italian campaign). He was an instructor and inspirer of others (authors, artists and soldiers) and he dug deeply into life, pouring forth the gathered materials of his experience with unremitting zeal. He coupled a particularly intensive struggle for universal harmony (the Napoleonic Code) with the greatest possible resort to particular, immediate and practical self-responsibility (as shown by his ability to succeed). He achieved uniquely through a development of unexpected experiences in life (e.g. in France and Egypt) and made his mark for good or evil. He overvalued the practical and had a tendency to meet many hardships. Heavy career demands made him doubt that he could succeed but his competitors had the same anxieties. He solved his problems by establishing goals and seeking them aggressively (e.g. the campaign in Italy). Imagination and psychism were brought to concrete use for money-making purposes (he exaggerated his actions in Italy to generate the most beneficial effect on the French public). Success stimulated further development and gave him some assurance of realising his goals (he moved on quickly from Italy). Important people recognised his abilities even if he couldn't (Saliceti, Barras, La Place, A. Robespierre, Tallyrand, etc.). As he grew older he learnt how to build in ways that were meaningful to his ultimate purpose, rather than labouring under the past illusion that he must conquer a world that was too formidable to master.

Late: He developed his love of power and leadership by his ability to organise, govern and rule others (developed during the Italian Campaign). He was fortunate regarding money and property (he donated a large amount of money to his mother) and further success came through foreign countries (Italy, Egypt, Austria, etc.) and through people from abroad. However, he would have felt most secure and comfortable working at home, or at least in familiar surroundings (i.e. in Paris).

Health

Napoleon was of somewhat short stature but had a muscular physique. His nervous system was relatively poor and his tendency was to overstrain through overdoing, or overexcitement, thereby impairing his vitality. He had good prospects for a long life but he was liable to rheumatism, to heart and to stomach troubles.

Reference: "Napoleon – The Path to Power: 1769 – 1799", P. Dwyer, Bloomsbury, London, UK, 2007.

CHAPTER 10

Julius Caesar

"Veni, vidi, vici."

Caesar was a Roman military and political leader. He played a critical role in the transformation of the Roman Republic into the Roman Empire.

As a politician he made use of popularist tactics. During the late 60s and into the 50s BC he formed political alliances that led to the so called "First Triumvirate", an extra-legal arrangement with Crassus and Pompey that lasted for several years. They were opposed by Cato, Bibulus and sometimes Cicero. Caesar's conquest of Gaul extended the Roman Empire to the North Sea and in 55 BC he also conducted the first Roman invasion of Britain. These achievements threatened to match Pompey's so that with the death of Crassus increased political tensions arose between the two survivors. When Caesar ordered his legions across the Rubicon in 49 BC he began a civil war from which he emerged as the unrivalled leader of the Roman world. He began extensive reforms of Roman society and government and centralised the bureaucracy of the Republic. A group of senators, led by Brutus, assassinated him in 44 BC, hoping to restore the Republic, but instead started another civil war. Shortly after the succession of Caesar's adopted nephew, Octavian -> Augustus, the Roman Senate in 42 BC officially sanctified Caesar as one of the Roman deities.

Julius Caesar - Horoscopes

Figure 9: Epoch Chart and Aspect Grid for Julius Caesar

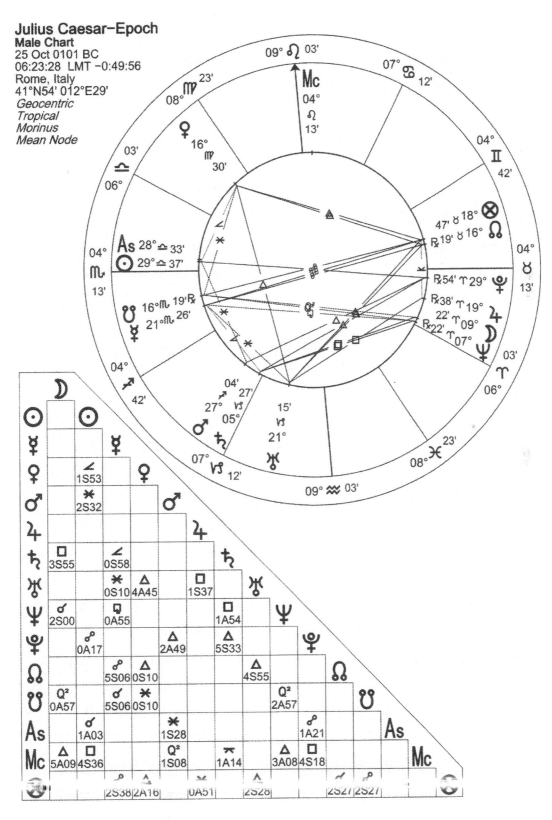

Caius Julius Caesar was born on the 13th July, 100 BC, near Rome, Italy, to Caius Julius Caesar, his father, and to Aurelia Cotta, his mother. What we are missing here is the time of birth. Bearing in mind the 1st Scorpio decanate predominance of our previous four power notables, we see that that the Sun can't be in Scorpio (it is in Cancer) leaving us with the possibilities that either the Morin Point or the Moon lie there. The everyday occurrence of the 1st decanate of Scorpio containing the Morin Point doesn't lead to an Epoch-Birth combination that fits Caesar properly. However, in the afternoon, the Moon entered the 1st Scorpio decanate and we find that there is a valid Epoch-Birth combination that seems to describe Caesar rather well, although, it is, of course, speculative. His Epoch*

- -

* At birth the Moon is above the Earth and increasing in light so that the Epoch is 1st Order. The Morin Point occupies a male area but the Moon lies in a negative (neutral) one, meaning that the Epoch is Regular.

+ Because the two planets inside the Earth's path in the Solar System, Venus and Mercury, have relatively small orbits, they cannot seem to get very far away from the Sun. Venus is never more than 48^0 away and Mercury is never more than 28^0 from the Sun. As a result, singleton cases for these three planets are essentially non-existent but just about possible for Venus, as in this case for Caesar's Epoch.

** Sharp-eyed readers may have noticed the absence of the planetoid Chiron from both Caesar's Birth and Epoch charts. This is not because Chiron did not exist then but rather that, around 700 A.D., it came so close to Saturn that its orbit around the Sun became changed significantly (see Chiron, the Swiss Ephemeris, the Internet). Whereas we know the position of Chiron with accuracy after that date, we have very little idea presently of its position before then.

Figure 10: Birth Chart and Aspect Grid for Julius Caesar.

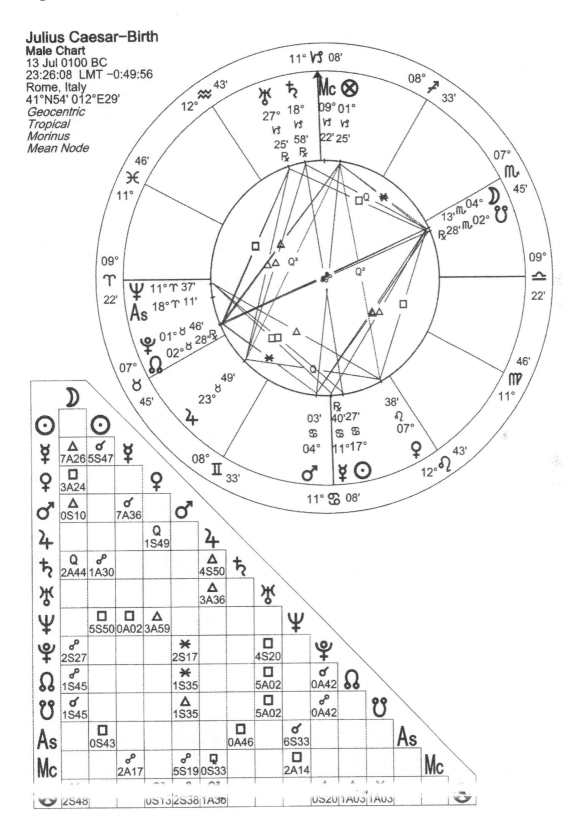

occurred on the 25th October, 101 BC, at nearly 06:25 a.m. The Sun was rising, right at the end of Libra, just above the Morin Point, in the 1st Scorpio decanate (see Figure 9), in strong opposition to Pluto (ruler) just at the end of Aries in the 7th House. This shows his ruthless behaviour towards others. This Sun – Pluto opposition forms the rim of an overall bucket shaping with singleton Venus+ as the anticlockwise handle planet in Virgo in the 11th House. Venus here signifies Caesar's extreme impatience without warm, human ties and his devotion to pleasure and the beautiful. Uranus trine Venus imparts a delightful and fascinating element to this devotion. The Sun in Libra – Moon in Aries polarity provides him with much mental ability and refinement while the Sun in 1st House – Moon in 6th House polarity gave him enough assertiveness to gain all that he desired. The Morin Point in the 1st Scorpio decanate supplies him with the selfish drive and capacity for hard work he needed to achieve while Pluto in the 7th House suggests that he had secret and ruthless enemies. Unlike the previous four power notables whose "good luck" comes from Jupiter's (the greater benefic) situation, Caesar's good luck would appear to stem from the special situation of Venus (the lesser benefic). 'Uncannily, at his Aunt Julia's funeral, Caesar confirmed that his family, the Julii, was descended from the goddess Venus!'

His Epoch generates the Birth chart and aspect grid shown in Figure 10.   Examination of both charts** shows that Caesar tended to be subjective rather than objective because most of the planets are below (North) the Earth (Morin Point). Both charts have a bucket shaping. For the Birth chart the Moon in Scorpio in the 8th House is the anticlockwise handle planet that shows Caesar's involvement with the public. The two buckets reveal the particular and uncompromising direction to his life-effort (towards power). Notice that the only special interplanetary aspect pattern occurs in the Birth chart as a distorted, fixed T-square having Uranus in Capricorn in the 11th House at the short end (focus) of the T. This means that he tended to put up with difficulties but with relief from Mars (ruler) in Cancer in the 4th House by expending energy caringly at home.

For the Birth chart, the Sun in Cancer – Moon in Scorpio polarity suggests the source of his pride and vindictiveness along with his love of display whereas the Sun in 4th House – Moon in 8th House polarity helped him to find satisfaction in his endeavours. The Sun opposition Saturn forms the rim of the bucket and indicates his limited self-expression and his heavy career demands. The Morin Point in Aries is responsible for his frank, impulsive tendencies but these were softened and so hidden by the influence of Neptune rising. Retrograde Mercury in Cancer in the 4th House indicates his fondness for childhood memories of security and the exact square to Neptune suggests that he became disorientated by life-changing situations.

Person Summary and Biographical Extracts

Character

General: Caesar's self-expression was hurtfully limited (his homosexual side was not really acceptable for a Roman leader). His life was hard and tended to cause self-pity. At his worst he had a criminal personality showing pride and vindictiveness especially where his feelings were concerned. His individuality, impulsiveness, daring (Caesar was a man of action), desire to reform, ability to revivify (Caesar's great knack was his ability to recover from setbacks), vigour, will-power and resourcefulness were all stimulated. He could be explosive and so likely to end situations and force new beginnings but with good results after a painful crisis. He had a frank, open outspoken and free-handed disposition. He was active, independent and aggressive (aged 19, Caesar won the "Civic Crown", Rome's highest award for gallantry) on the surface but at heart quiet, harmonious, affectionate, tractable, courteous and retiring (Caesar's charm won over the Roman crowds, the legionnaires and many aristocratic women).   At times he was impatient and lacking in perseverance but assertive enough to gain all that he wanted. Sometimes his happiness was secret.

Mentality;   For Caesar, reason, perception, great sensitivity, prudence and intuition were all well-blended with a large amount of mental refinement and much ability in all mental activities (Caesar was brighter and more capable than the overwhelming majority of the other senators).   He was fond of acquiring knowledge, intellectual pursuits, debate, argument and always being at the front. 'Caesar was a prolific letter writer and author – writing "De Analogia" in 54 BC while in Gaul along with his "Commentaries".' "Clouds of glory" were to be expected (Caesar was raised to think of himself as special) rather than any delusion. He should have acted on his ideas and hunches (which he did). Strongly emotional, subtle, poetical, changeable and full of involved schemes and plans, his vivid imagination could be gullible and confused so that, at times, his mind was not well-directed. 'Caesar misjudged the public mood both in Gaul and in Rome.' He felt confusion between dominance and submissiveness (his relationship with Nicomedes seemingly was one of submission [the "female" partner], i.e. he was the "Queen of Bithynia"), in which initiative battled against emotional insecurity. In fact, these emotional contradictions helped him to express himself properly in cases where he was positively sure of himself. He was comfortable absorbing all that had represented past resources of security so that his thoughts were centred on the feelings he had met in his early years even though he thought that his family's needs held him back. Resulting touchiness induced escapism.

Lifestyle: He kept trying to recreate his childhood and because of this his upbringing had been important. He did not fully appreciate the idea of growth and kept thinking that he was incapable of letting go earlier phases of his life. Having a responsive, amiable and good disposition he learnt something from everyone he contacted. 'There was a generosity about Caesar's behaviour that was unmatched by any other Roman who came to power in similar circumstances.' He often said more than he meant to, being enthusiastic, energetic, enterprising, progressive and aspiring. He tended to complain about why his life was not blossoming the way he thought it should. He was apt to be too yielding under pressure and inclined to lean on others (e.g. Labienus felt that he deserved much of the credit for some of Caesar's successes). He also tended to let difficulties remain as they were, and so put up with them, thereby becoming patiently conditioned to trying circumstances, but not without nervous strain. He got relief from strain through his desire to work for the care of others, at home, with energy, in quick and able ways. Indeed, he was grateful for any opportunity to show how much he cared about people (Caesar's whole career was based on trying to win friends rather than to destroy enemies). Despite this he often complained that he didn't have enough time to take care of his own needs and resented the fact that others expected him to do everything. As he was self-confident, he didn't need to defend himself by stating that he was, or by complaining that everyone else was unqualified or untrained. He proved himself by being satisfied.

He was extremely impatient without warm or commonplace ties and was passionately devoted to pleasure, or the experience of the beautiful, in every phase of human relationships. 'For much of his life Caesar was an enthusiastic collector of fine art, gems and pearls (an expensive hobby for a young man).'

Ambitious (he fought a civil war when his rivals were determined to end his career and so won supreme power using military force), he rarely missed opportunities; neither was he thwarted by obstacles nor failure. He dug deeply into life and poured forth the result of his gathered experiences with unremitting zeal. Part of his life-plan was to show that he had plenty of ideas for achieving an abundant life-style. His obsession was power with a compelling need to achieve emancipation (e.g. his law of land resettlement during his consulship of 59 BC).

There was also a tendency to retirement, to philanthropy and to day-dreaming.

Relationships

Others: There was a love of display with success in magical and psychic affairs but his magnetism was easily stimulated towards the sensational.

He had a vital need to co-operate and did more for others than he did for himself. He was good at activities that allowed him to show his skills in handling people such as achieving smooth working of any club, society or group. 'There is little doubt that Caesar's campaigns ran better when he was at the helm.' As an instructor and inspirer of others he achieved much power and influence over them. He stimulated people to become independent enough to succeed eventually without him (e.g. Octavian). He left a lasting impression on others by his sacrifices. However, by reforming others he failed to see himself clearly. He sought fulfilment of his personal aims without regard for the feelings of others and so tended to advance himself through ruthless behaviour towards them. Thus he became emotionally at odds with others, who seemed unable to accomplish anything without his help. While he resented this intrusion on his time and energy he was, nevertheless, psychologically dependent on the people he met in his professional affairs, who gave him the opportunity to show just how competent he really was. Thus he had great obstacles to overcome in his relationships with others and he tried to transform what others thought about him. His enemies were secret and ruthless.

In later years he would have developed a beautiful rapport with children, which would have turned out to be one of his greatest strengths (but it was not to be, except possibly with Octavian. However, the boy pharaoh, Ptolemy XIII, deceived him).

<u>Friends:</u> Caesar was happy among like-minded friends.

<u>Family:</u> The frustration he felt with his parents should have given him the ambition to succeed on his own merits. An early death or separation from, a parent (his father died when Caesar was 16) is indicated.

He didn't need to have devoted so much time to his career that his partner and children were denied the pleasure of his attention and mutual interests. He wanted his children to enjoy the best and to become self-reliant when pursuing their own destinies (which his daughter, Julia, did).

<u>Lover:</u> His affection was cool, undemonstrative and critical but with a retiring, modest charm. There was unusualness in his expression of love, or in artistic accomplishment for that matter, that was delightful, intriguing and fascinating. There was an easy shifting away from one attraction and the quick-forming of another. Partings were likely but for good reasons and with pleasant replacements or reunions. He wanted a partner who needed him and who was also supportive of his goals, someone to whom he could turn when he faced reversals, yet who would allow him to stand on his own when conditions improved (e.g. Cornelia, Servilia and possibly Cleopatra). Elopement with a self-sufficient partner is indicated. His marriage should have given him comfort and contentment so that he could have applied himself more completely to the demands of his career but unconsciously he disrupted the harmony he sought in marriage. Thus an inharmonious marriage was probable (he divorced Pompeia).

Career

<u>Early:</u>   He followed his parents closely both in character and occupation. He may have become conditioned to repressing his creative imagination and he may have preferred to indulge his parents in their desires. He may have looked for a way to use his talent at home to work for the care of others and to collect and maintain both family and home. At first it wasn't easy for him to express himself except in ways that would have offended his parents. His upbringing had given him an understanding of human frailty (as experienced during the civil, social and slave wars of his youth as well as during the horror of proscriptions) and serving others only enhanced him in his career. Later, he realised that unless he resisted his family he would never get an opportunity to make a life of his own. He had amazing sources of inspiration but he needed training to exploit his creative talent (for his time Caesar was well-educated) for optimum results. If he had been able to develop his talent, he would have been freer to choose the field of activity he wanted. His fate was precipitated by his impatience and head-strong tendencies as well as by his fearless, pioneering and progressive spirit. Possibly a great change occurred and an entirely new environment and occupation was taken up.   Probably he had to break with the past to improve on his early circumstances but his future required it. He had an ability to work and to push-on in life. He could have succeeded in any career that brought him before the public, such as counselling, financial consulting, and medicine. In these cases he would have been stimulated to a high degree of proficiency and excellence. As he followed this direction there would have been intrusions on the time he wanted for personal indulgences but the satisfaction he got more than compensated for his loss of personal pleasure.

<u>Middle:</u> His highly developed psychic ability served him well as he sought to fulfil his potential. His inner and outer worlds were well-co-ordinated, which helped him to derive satisfaction from his endeavours. The institutions that society had set up were the very thing he needed to make him vibrate to the essence of life itself. He kept to himself any doubts about his ability to cope with challenging situations because he would have been ashamed for people to have known about his weaknesses (e.g. epilepsy). Heavy career demands may have made him doubt that he could succeed but his competitors had the same anxieties. He resolved his doubts by establishing goals and seeking them aggressively. Important people recognised his talent even if he couldn't (Sulla said that in Caesar there were many Mariuses). Honest success was achieved, providing criminal tendencies were resisted, by means of a thrusting, purposeful nature coupled with a capacity for hard work. Instead of trying to match everyone's performance, which he probably overestimated, he developed his talent to the utmost so that he could have accepted any challenge knowing that he would be able to succeed. In this way he would earn a good living needed to offset his great need for security. There was a particular and uncompromising direction to his life-effort (towards power) with no concern over end results or to conserve either himself or his resources. He adapted his allegiances to lines along which he could make his efforts count for the most. However, he was rather unfortunate in his affairs through his life being subject to upsets and forced new phases. He didn't receive the services he required unless he asked for them but he would rather not have done that because it embarrassed him. He didn't let his feelings of responsibility to his family and loved ones prevent him from fulfilling his needs. If he had had to devote as much time to others as he did to satisfy his own needs he would have become bitter because he would have accomplished little of lasting value for himself. By paying attention to his own need to develop he

eliminated the danger of insecurity in his later years. He had a developed sense of social obligation (towards emancipation) and the rewards that others derived from his efforts were both significant and valuable (businessmen supported him because he was considered to be a good risk).

Late: His preoccupation with financial security gave people confidence that he could help them with their business affairs. They believed that he would serve their interests well because he had a great deal of self-confidence. He himself wanted to accumulate enough money to make investments and so assure his future financial independence.

Health

Appearance: Caesar was of moderate height with a straight and upright walk. 'He was slightly built but made up for this by determination.' He had a fair complexion, light brown hair and possibly full-blue eyes that, at times, had a dreamy or introspective look to them, or withdrawn expression. This tended to soften his positive manner and appearance. 'Caesar had a somewhat high-pitched voice'.

Health: He had excellent strength both physically and emotionally but tended to exhaust himself completely because he burned up energy so rapidly. As a result he needed to take time to recuperate. He would have had a love for athletics and success in gymnastic affairs because his spine and muscular system were very supple. 'Caesar would ride his horse with his hands behind its back controlling it completely just by using his knees.' He would have had some liability to head troubles and a tendency to falls, chills and to orthopaedic problems. 'Caesar was abstemious about alcohol.' 'Living rough, while fleeing from Sulla, he contracted malaria.' 'He suffered from epilepsy from aged 30.' Astrologically there are several indicators for this condition but a strong Scorpio emphasis coupled with Neptune rising in exact square to Mercury (retrograde) is consistent with this.

Reference: "Caesar – the Life of a Colossus", A. Goldsworthy, Weidenfeld & Nicholson, Orion Publishing Group, London, 2006.

- -

CHAPTER 11

Alexander the Great

"Never Knowingly Defeated in Battle"

Alexander the Great (356-323 BC) (father: Philip II, mother Olympias [a mystical woman, violent and headstrong when provoked] of Epirus) was an ancient Greek king (336-323 BC) of Macedon. He was one of the most successful military commanders ever. By the time of his death, he had conquered the Persian Empire, adding it to Macedon's European territories. This was most of the world as known to the ancient Greeks.

Following the death of his father, Philip II, he confirmed Macedonian rule by quashing a rebellion of southern Greek states as well as by subduing Macedon's northern neighbours. Now Alexander set out east against the Persian Empire, which he defeated and overthrew. His conquests included Anatolia, the Levant, Egypt, Bactria, Mesopotamia and extensions as far as the Punjab, India. Before his death he had made plans for expansion into Arabia after which he proposed to advance west to Carthage, Rome and the Iberian Peninsula. However, his original vision had been to the east, to the ends of the world and to the Great Outer Sea, as described by his boyhood tutor and mentor, Aristotle.

Alexander integrated many foreigners into his army in a "Policy of Fusion". He also encouraged marriages between his soldiers and foreigners and married two foreign princesses himself.

Alexander died after twelve years of constant military campaigning, possibly the combined result of malaria, poisoning, typhoid fever, viral encephalitis and alcoholism. Alexander has featured prominently throughout history and his exploits have inspired others to become heroes, like he did, in the tradition of Achilles.

Alexander-the-Great – Horoscopes

There are three items of data required to cast a natal horoscope: 1) the time, 2) the date and 3) the place, of birth. Nowadays the item of data missing in English speaking countries is the time of birth. However, in ancient times, for those for whom we have any data at all, it is the date of birth, rather than the time, that we lack. Ancient scribes, recording important births, often provided clues from which we can deduce a reasonable birth time. The overriding difficulty is to determine the actual date of birth with confidence. For example, a century ago, we thought that Alexander the Great was born on the 1st July 357 BC at 9:30 in the evening[16] at Pella, Macedon, Greece. Now, historians are just about certain that the actual date was 20th July, 356 BC, i.e. over a year later. If we combine the time of birth used a century ago with the presently accepted birth date, we may be able to cast a valid horoscope for Alexander. A preliminary birth chart shows that the Sun was close to 27⁰ Cancer, the Moon was close to 5⁰ Sagittarius and the Morin Point was close to 22⁰ Pisces. The Regular Epoch* from this occurred on the 28th October, 357 BC at 8:00 a.m. The overall shaping of the chart (see Figure 11) indicates a mixture of two "Bucket" shapes combined with a "Splay" type. The first, anticlockwise handle consists of the triple conjunction of Jupiter with Venus and Neptune, with the Sun opposition Saturn as the bucket rim. The second, clockwise handle consists of Saturn with the Moon opposition Neptune as the rim, while the planets generally could be considered as three irregular groupings. This means that Alexander had a particular direction to his life effort and that he tended to be a

Figure 11: Epoch Chart and Aspect Grid for Alexander the Great.

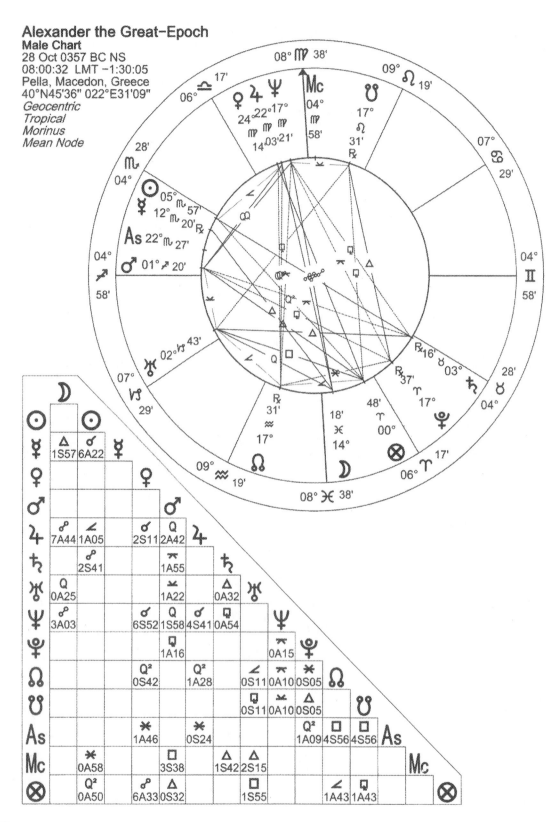

unique individual who exercised control impulsively just when it was needed. The Sun in Scorpio - Moon in Pisces polarity shows restlessness and anxiety, whereas the Sun in the 12th House – Moon in the 4th House polarity suggests the need for him to develop his creativity into useful skills. The Sun opposition Saturn indicates that his artistic self-expression was hurtfully limited and the Moon opposition Neptune shows sensitivity but also deception and gullibility. The Morin Point in Sagittarius provided him with his honourable, generous character while Mars rising in Sagittarius gave him his invincibility. Jupiter (the ruler) becomes doubly important as the central, handle planet of the triple conjunction in Virgo in the 10th House and emphasises his quiet desire for scope in life and his success in acquiring it.

- -

*At birth the Moon was above the Earth and increasing in light so that his Epoch was 1st Order. Inspection of Bailey's Table of Sex Degrees (see Table 1, Ch. 1) shows that both the Moon and the Morin Point lie in Male areas, making the Epoch a Sex one. In this case there are three, possible, valid Epochs for a male birth: a regular Epoch and two, irregular variations (1st and 2nd). The 1st variation, irregular Epoch is very unlikely because it fails to indicate Alexander's strong vitality and zest for exploration. To decide which of the other two fits him best we need to take account of his physical deformity, namely scoliosis of the neck (Potts' disease), which may also explain his reportedly short stature. Consulting Cornell's Encyclopaedia of Medical Astrology[13] shows that this disease occurs when the Sun lies in a fixed sign and is badly aspected by Saturn from the 6th House. The regular Epoch satisfies this requirement (Sun in Scorpio in the 12th House opposite to Saturn in Taurus in the 6th House). The regular Epoch is also the more likely one because it leads to a longer gestation time that occurs more frequently for a first birth.

Figure 12: Birth Chart and Aspect Grid for Alexander the Great.

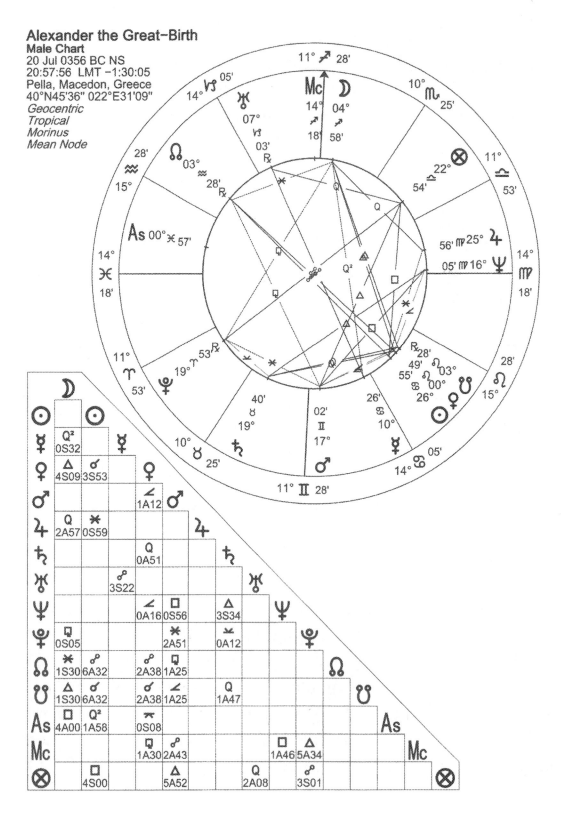

The Epoch generates the Ideal Birth chart and aspect grid shown in Figure 12. The overall shaping of this chart is of the "Splash" type that shows his genuine, universal width of interest. As with the Epoch chart there are no Special Interplanetary Aspect Patterns save, perhaps, for Venus lying bi-semisquare between Mars and Neptune. The Sun in Cancer – Moon in Sagittarius polarity shows that his emotional and devotional nature were stimulated while the Sun in the 6th House – Moon in 10th House polarity indicates that his need for personal satisfaction has to be combined with better fulfilment for others. The Sun conjoint Venus tends to impart effeminacy, while the sextile to Jupiter gives good luck. The Moon in close sesquiquadrate to Pluto shows that he was subject to upsets and to forced new phases in life. His Morin Point in Pisces provides him with a strongly artistic personality and Neptune (the ruler) in Virgo in the 7th House shows that his idealism would tend to be weak, that there would be peculiar conditions connected with partnership and that hard work done for idealistic ends probably would prove disappointing. There are no planets rising in his Birth chart.

Once again both Alexander's charts must remain speculative although their combined interpretation seems to fit him well. Note also that the planetoid Chiron is absent from both charts as explained previously.

Person Summary and "In Search of Alexander" Extracts

Character

General: Alexander was a (famously) generous, honourable (he loved to reward the right kind of spirit) character, who inspired respect. Although he had a tendency to be impractical he was a real instructor and inspirer of others (he aroused worship but, at times, was also impossible to deal with). He was cheerful, affectionate, warm-hearted, sympathetic and charitable, even perhaps deriving benefit from these qualities in others. Although contented with his own surroundings and ways his emotional and devotional nature was stimulated generating a strongly artistic personality with an interest in ideology and psychism. His artistic self-expression would have been through his affections, through beauty and through gentle ways. Thus he tended towards effeminacy but he had sufficient ambition and intellectual power to rise through merit and adaptability. This other side felt invincible, rebellious, aspiring and talkative. 'A murderous fighter, he showed bravery bordering on folly at the front line, sharing every hardship, decision and the toughest labour.' As a quick worker and stimulating in action he could accomplish much in a short time (with a brusque manner went discipline, speed and shrewd, political sense) but with tendencies towards explosion (he murdered Cleitus, one of his "companions" after provocation), antagonism and with a need to end conditions and force new beginnings (he seldom gave a second chance). Overall he was a unique individual showing a particular yet impersonal temperament that could not be limited easily to any steady point of application. Throughout his short life his artistic self-expression was hurtfully limited due to continuous military campaigns. He had a love of the sea and animals (he loved his dog and especially his horse, Bucephalus).

Mentality: At best he had a capacity for genuine, universal interest, or, at worst, was one who scattered his interests far too widely. 'He had wide interests, such as hunting, reading, food, architecture of cities, agriculture, irrigation and patronised art, music, drama and dancing.' He was very restless, anxious, mentally active, imaginative and sensitive but with good commonsense and nervous force. He had a tendency to be enthusiastic for cheerful ways of enjoyment and all-out for far-flung, exaggerated and "off at a tangent" ideas, which may have seemed inspirational but probably were better off well scrutinised. To compensate, there was also a tendency for these ideas to be kept in bounds and judged for their practicality. He also had a tendency to be self-righteous and priggish (as well as impatient and conceited). His mind was mathematical, which strengthened his critical faculties and helped his self-conscious preparedness but made his idealism weak through critical coolness. Because he was psychic, with abilities for prophesy, inspirational speaking and dream retention, mediumship was easy for him but so too was moral weakness. Thus he was inclined towards deceit, duplicity (he altered a letter from Darius III so that his "companions" would reject it) and gullibility that lessened his methodical tendencies. On the other hand he could be economical and useful, thereby increasing his persistency and giving him the ability to use his virtues rather than his vices.

Actually his unusually keen mind worked best when focussed on the spiritual journey. He would keep reviewing to find the depths of things that others had overlooked. He was capable of rediscovering that which had been buried in the past, making him a natural for anything of a scientific nature (he recalled military tactics used long ago). As a deep individual he was fully capable of solving his own problems but turned most of his thoughts inward to try to understand the nature of his own being. He perceived a continuance of past ideas concerning the relationships of things, people and circumstances in the universe. At the personality level he became introverted but he was thinking all the time. He would replay past conversations for days and weeks after their actual occurrence. He could have become mystically orientated. Possibly he would have had great musical ability as words, for him, seemed an inadequate form of expression.

Lifestyle: Alexander was good at starting new enterprises (the difficulty was making him stop). He was able to stand strongly, in part due to separation from a loved one (his father died when Alexander was young) and so carried something of an inner loneliness that only strengthened his individuality. He developed strong ideas to move ahead into areas as yet unknown to him (e.g. into India as a curious explorer). This desire for more unusual and unconventional scope in his life was expressed in quiet, unassuming ways. He was fond of travelling, exploring new scenes, new thoughts, new ideas and pleasurable activities, particularly those involving the outdoor life. 'He came less to change than to inherit and to restore.' As a result he found success in foreign affairs (in Persia and in Egypt) and in religious matters (he developed his "policy of fusion"). There was a tendency for him to concentrate on visions of the future (e.g. he showed wide insight into economic realities by planning to open the sea route from India to the Red Sea), rather than of the present. Control, for him, tended to be impulsive and to respond to an immediate, rather than future need (which, nevertheless, he planned for carefully). He was more on the silent side but could become destructive (e.g. the sack of Thebes) when he saw things that didn't live up to his idealistic expectations. There was an awkward certainty to every approach he made to the problems of life (he was not to be crossed, or to be told what to do, having firm views about exactly what he wanted). His sensitivity gave him a keen internal aspiration to become a channel through which good forces could flow. He dug deeply into life and poured forth the result of his gathered experiences with unremitting zeal but with no desire to conserve either himself or his resources. 'His ideals pitched his life too high to last. He lived for the ideal of a distant past (as lived by Homer's Achilles) striving to realise an age, in which he had been too late to share.'

He experienced long periods of mental depression as he tried to understand himself at the deepest of levels. Accordingly he spent much time away from many outer world activities that would have prevented him from seeing himself and so concentrated his attention on the deep mysteries that confronted his inner mind. He was a student of the past and could have become an excellent metaphysician, tending towards a very dogmatic and secular religion, if he had been able to direct his mental energies towards universal knowledge.

Relationships

Others: Alexander's deep sense of devotion to others came from his early religious training. 'He was courteous to women and honoured the captured Persian queen after the battle of Issus.' As he was almost always misunderstood by others, he underestimated himself and tended to retreat from life. He could be suspicious of others, shrewd and tactless, but a truth seeker at all costs. Additionally he had to be careful about showing his creativity so that his competitors couldn't copy it for their own ends. However, popularity and much social life were likely to have resulted from the widening of the scope of his desire to form harmonious relationships with others. Importantly for him (as the hero), he had to know that others considered him to be indispensable. This being so (none of his "companions" had his combination of qualities and they knew it), his efforts brought him much spiritual fulfilment.

Friends and Family: Offspring were favoured and he may have derived benefit by children and by friends. Although it might have been difficult, he would have managed to satisfy his responsibilities to his children and still have had a career that satisfied his desire to achieve recognition for his services.

Partner: A disappointing childhood may have conditioned him to escape into marriage, which was hardly the best reason for such a demanding relationship. He might have chosen someone who was as insecure as he was, out of sentimental pity.

Although love affairs were numerous, confusion occurred and even deception. Thus partnerships were disappointing, unreliable and possibly secret. He wanted people to understand him and to listen to his romantic fantasies including his dream of finding the right person to help him to exploit his creativity. His partner was likely to have been spiritually minded or artistic but difficulties arose through these and disillusion developed. He could be sexually detached, lacking the warmth that others might have expected at the sexual level. Alternatively, he could also get himself sexually preoccupied at the mental level. Despite all this he was better in partnership than alone. His partner was the catalyst that made him excel in his efforts. His partner gave him support when he met problems and approval when he did his job well. Conversely his devotion inspired his partner to assist him so that they both benefitted in the life they shared. 'Hephaestion, son of Amyntas and one of Alexander's co-pupils with Aristotle, was an ideal partner for Alexander, just like Patroclus was for Achilles.' Overall, there were peculiar conditions about ("mixed") marriage/partnerships or a hidden arrangement about these.

Career

Early: For Alexander life was hard, causing him self-pity (his artistic side had had to be repressed). It wasn't easy for him to be realistic about making his own life. 'Homer's Achilles provided him with an appealing model to follow.' If he could have accepted responsibility for finding a way to earn a good living, the financial rewards would have given him security and would have compensated for any emotional anxiety. His most urgent priority was to make the necessary investment to turn his creativity into useful skills to enable him to succeed in his career. To be rewarding, he had to begin as soon as possible (he had several tutors). His success in striving for significance depended on how well he used his creativity. Self-development was the key (Aristotle wrote several guidance pamphlets for him). He would have become a credit to himself by building a sound mind in a healthy body. He might have been unlucky, thwarted or showed more promise than performance. In addition, his sensitivity would have slowed his progress unless he had learnt to assert himself. He had to be both gregarious and demanding if necessary (which he became) to achieve the goals he had set up. Others would not have felt threatened because he was always considerate of their feelings. If he had reached out to help less fortunate people he would have learnt how competent he was in coping with the world. However, his keen imagination helped him to become independent. Additionally feelings of stress spurred him on to better fulfilment (he felt that he had to live up to his father's high example). There were excellent indications for success in the affairs of the world, e.g. in business, or in professional, political or social life. There was ease of accomplishment through plenty of opportunities in life and the feeling that good luck was to be expected (which he over-trusted eventually, e.g. by marching into the Makran desert). He had the dramatic ability to arouse people to correct social injustice (he was able to harangue his troops successfully). As a low-key catalyst he was able to accomplish a great deal without attracting much attention. It wasn't really in his nature to be violent but he got the job done just the same. His desire to gain satisfaction in his achievements was balanced by a desire to help others seek fulfilment in their own desires. Thus he was reasonably centred on doing what he had to do to gain and to hold the position he wanted, and he knew how to use his creativity to ensure continued growth in his career (he inspired by example and by reward). He could have been effective in politics at the local or national level, building construction, design, environmental enterprises, land management, natural resources, real-estate or in the creative arts such as acting, dancing, painting or sculpture. A little training would have revealed his enormous potential that could have been used even in an undeveloped state with success.

<u>Middle:</u> He had a particular and uncompromising direction to his life-effort (the curious explorer) even though he was subject to upsets that resulted in forced new phases. He adapted his allegiances to lines along which he could make his efforts count for the most (even to managing his huge empire once he had got it). He had the ability to assess what the public needed and required of him and the expertise to promote himself so that he was often the one chosen for the task. Making the most of his potential came easily to him and he had an unmistakable glow when he knew he had done the right thing (such as realising that the ruling class of his empire required both Persians and Macedonians). Despite this he may not have derived the full benefit because it was so natural to him. Some circumstances in his life must have exerted pressure on him (probably from Hephaestion and/or his wives). He had to find ways to translate his imaginative ideas into worthwhile activity. He always thought that his goals were just around the next corner, which may have been true, but the chances were that he had already accomplished more than most other people in similar circumstances (which was also true). He needed not to have forgotten his benefactors (which he tried to do) and he should have learnt to be content with each achievement (which he found very difficult). Additionally his career may have caused some problems in personal relationships if his partner resented the time and attention he devoted to it. Thus there could well have been ungratified ambition and a difficulty in rising into his proper sphere. Very hard work may have been done for idealistic ends (his "policy of fusion" was not popular with his fellow Macedonians). The results may have been disappointing and elusive because all was too imaginary. Business affairs should have been as foolproof as possible in that he needed to have a binding contract before he agreed to provide any service. Nevertheless he could have succeeded by being self-employed so that his earnings depended on his self-determination

and ingenuity. He could have provided almost any high-priced service that people required. The public would have got what they paid for because he would have had to live with himself if the job hadn't met with his own high standards. He should have let the world benefit from his talent, while he gained fulfilment and profit as well.

Eventually, irregular (e.g. dressing in Persian clothes), over-glamorous (he ordered huge monuments to be built to Hephaestion and to his father), escapist (after setbacks he became too fond of drinking celebrations) ways would have brought about his downfall.

Health

'He showed extraordinary toughness, probably inherited from his father. Nine wounds were sustained in battle including a broken ankle, thigh wounds, a bolt of a catapult through his shoulder, stoned on the head and neck but most seriously by an arrow through his chest that pierced his lung. Understandably he never fully recovered from this. He also had the ability to withstand the desert (both Makran and Libyan [to Siwah]). He had a strong gaze (because he believed in himself?).'

He had a responsive nervous system but strange fears played on his nerves. His health could have been undermined by these and by a susceptibility to fish-poisoning or by harm from impure water (bad water from the river Cydnus at Tarsus gave him a fever; impure water near Babylon could well have been responsible for his death). There was also a tendency to falls, chills and orthopaedic problems, e.g. Potts' disease (see earlier).

Reference: "Alexander the Great", R. Lane Fox, Penguin, London, 2nd Ed., 2004.

- -

CHAPTER 12

Summary

1) <u>Sign Decanate Distributions Among the Three Main Chart Indicators:</u> There are three main indicators for interpretation for either Epoch or Birth charts; these are the positions of the Sun, of the Moon and of the Morin Point. Table 1 assembles this data for our six, 1st tier, power notables.

<u>Table 1:</u> The Sign Decanates containing the Sun, Moon and Morin Point for the Epoch and Birth Charts of the Six Power Notables.

	< - - - - - - - - - - - Epoch- - - - - ->< - - - - - - - - - Birth - - - - - - - ->					
Name	**Sun**	**Moon**	**MoPo**	**Sun**	**Moon**	**MoPo**
Edward III	1st Aquarius	3rd Taurus	1st Scorpio	3rd Scorpio	1st Taurus	3rd Scorpio
A Hitler	3rd Leo	1st Scorpio	1st Capricorn	1st Taurus	1st Capricorn	1st Scorpio
J Stalin	1st Pisces	1st Scorpio	1st Aries	3rd Sagittarius	1st Libra	1st Scorpio
Napoleon	1st Scorpio	3rd Aries	3rd Cancer	3rd Leo	3rd Capricorn	3rd Libra
J Caesar	3rd Libra	1st Aries	1st Scorpio	3rd Cancer	1st Scorpio	1st Aries
Alexander the Great	1st Scorpio	2nd Pisces	1st Sagittarius	3rd Cancer	1st Sagittarius	2nd Pisces

Table 1 shows that the 1st decanate of Scorpio occurs significantly more often than any of the others. All six notables have at least one entry and Hitler, Stalin and Caesar have two, although these occur because the Order of their Epochs requires this. Those born of this decanate are reserved, shrewd, secretive and proud. Since all six notables are strong characters they would also have been prudent, self-controlled and highly dignified as well as penetrative, mystical and intelligent. Several decanates don't appear at all.

2) <u>Overall Planetary Shaping:</u>

<u>Table 2:</u> Overall Planetary Shaping of the Epoch and Birth Charts of the Six Power Notables.

Name	Epoch	Birth
Edward III	Bucket (Chiron handle)	See-Saw
A Hitler	Bowl	Splay
J Stalin	Bucket (Uranus handle)	Locomotive
Napoleon	See-Saw	Bucket (Uranus/Chiron handles)
J Caesar	Bucket (Venus handle)	Bucket (Moon handle)
Alexander the Great	2 Buckets (Venus/Jupiter and Saturn/Pluto handles)	Splash

Table 2 shows that the most prevalent shaping is the bucket. All six notables have at least one of these except Hitler, who has a closely related bowl shaping. The interpretation for a bucket shaping is: A particular and rather uncompromising direction to the life effort. There is interest in a cause (like a bowl [Hitler] that sacrifices everything for an ideal) but with much less concern over end results. Also there is no basic desire to conserve the self or its resources. The bucket person is apt to adapt his allegiances to lines along which he can make his efforts count for the most. This person is best as an instructor/inspirer of others or, at worst, an agitator/malcontent. He digs deeply into life and pours forth the fruits of his gathered experiences with unremitting zeal.

3) <u>Special Interplanetary Aspect Patterns:</u> Apart from Caesar and Alexander the Great, the notables had kite formations in either their Epoch or Birth charts. KEIII had a fanhandle in his birth chart in which Jupiter in Taurus in the 7th House was the focal planet, together with a weak, askew, biquintile kite in his birth chart. Neither Caesar nor Alexander had kites in their charts but Alexander had his Sun – Venus conjunction in his birth chart as the central focus of a bi-semisquare pattern. Napoleon had a Grand Trine kite in his

Birth chart and Stalin not only had both a sesquiquadrate and a tredecile kite in his Birth chart but also a tredecile kite in his Epoch chart.

Examples of external relief of personality strain derived from the cross-bar of a kite by easing aspects to its ends are present. Thus KEIII's Chiron in Virgo in the 11th House is sextile to the Sun and trine to Jupiter across the fanhandle pattern in his Birth chart. Activities involving Chiron's influence should provide a source of ease from the strain in the fanhandle's opposition. Again, the trine to the Sun in Taurus in the 7th House provides ease and suggests ways for the personality strain in the Chiron-Moon/Jupiter opposition in Hitler's Birth chart. On the other hand the T-square formed by the Sun across the tredecile kite in Stalin's Epoch chart considerably aggravates an already stressful, personal situation derived from the Moon-Neptune opposition. Finally, the Grand Trine of Uranus-Venus-Neptune in Stalin's Birth chart could well provide a route to some personal ease, at one end of the short cross-bar, from the strain from the Moon-Pluto opposition of his tredecile kite.

There are additional special interplanetary aspect patterns of note in these charts. Thus Napoleon has two Grand Trines in his Epoch chart: one comprising Neptune-Pluto-Mars/Uranus conjunction and the second Saturn-Chiron-Mercury/Venus conjunction. Adolf Hitler's Epoch chart contains a mutable/fixed T-square formed by Venus at the midpoint of the Jupiter-(Pluto/Neptune conjunction) opposition (see Appendix 2a [2]). Similarly Caesar's fixed T-square in his Birth chart finds ease from the aspects that Mars makes to the Moon-Pluto opposition while the Sun-Pluto opposition in his Epoch chart also finds ease from the aspects it receives from Mars.

4) <u>General Interpretation:</u> The six power notables were expected to have a lucky journey through life, although this could be hard. They all had trouble with women. Their partnerships were not easy so that life, at times, was solitary, during which they could concentrate

on pursuing their careers. They could all adopt a criminal personality through the Scorpio influence and were all unconcerned by the deaths of countless thousands of enemy soldiers as well as of their own. They were all sensitive so that they could read character well, but could themselves be vulnerable also. Moreover they all had a retrograde, personal planet in their charts, which tends to make them out-of-touch in that particular principal of personality, although Jupiter, for KEIII, is unusual.

5) <u>Biographical Similarities:</u> They all had to establish themselves early on at critical stages in their careers. Thus KEIII had to stabilise the English monarchy. Hitler felt he had to rescue Germany following the aftermath of World War I. Alexander had to stabilise Greece and assert himself following the sudden death of his father in battle. Napoleon had to save France after the French revolution and Stalin did the same for Russia after its revolution. Caesar felt obliged to resort to civil war to achieve his (benevolent) dictatorship. In terms of degree of rise, Hitler rose the most, closely followed by Stalin, by Napoleon and then by Caesar. Both Edward III and Alexander were born with silver spoons in their mouths and both received the benefits of private education. In terms of scale Stalin probably achieved the most, lived the longest and was responsible for the most deaths. Napoleon probably achieved a little more than Hitler and Caesar, and they perhaps more than Edward III, who outlived all three. Alexander achieved a great deal but died before he was able to consolidate all his gains (and continue to the West?). His empire disintegrated not long after his death.

6) <u>Conclusions:</u> All six power notables have significant Epoch and Birth charts, the combined interpretations of which seem to fit each one, individually, quite well, even to the extent of showing how each one was capable of achieving what he did. We could conclude that a potentially great leader would have the first decanate of Scorpio featured strongly in his charts, which should contain an overall

bucket shaping together with interplanetary aspect patterns within their two charts. They should be lucky in general but unfortunate in their love lives so that they could work hard on their military/political/social careers. Also, distressing circumstances need to surround them so that their talents can come to the fore. In other words, "Cometh the hour, cometh the man" sounds appropriate. The character of these power notables is clearly an important factor but so too is the prevailing environment at the time of their individual primes.

Probably Astrology can contribute significantly to our understanding of great and (in)famous leaders in just the same way that it also can to our own personal characters particularly when using the combined method shown here.

7) 2nd Tier, Power Notables: Let's now consider nine, perhaps slightly lesser (2nd Tier) power notables (for whom we have also good birth data!) to see how well our conclusions can be relied on. Appendix 4 presents the Epoch and Birth charts together with their aspect grids for the last six notables. Table 3 lists all nine of them in time and contains their Epoch and Birth data as well as the Order and Type of their Epochs.

Table 3: Epoch and Birth Dates, Times and Places for 2nd Tier, Power Notables.

Name	Epoch Date	Epoch Time	Order and Type of Epoch
Cicero	21/3/107 BC	14:54:38	2nd; Sex, Irreg. 3rd Var.
Nero	23/2/37 AD	06:17:52	2nd; Irreg. 2nd Var.
Domitian	6/2/51 AD	01:36:32	1st; Sex, Regular
Henry VIII	22/9/1490 NS	18:00:36	2nd; Sex, Irreg. 1st Var.
Philip II (E)	15/8/1526 OS	04:45:48	4th; Sex, Regular
Elizabeth I	29/12/1532 OS	13:31:04	4th; Sex, Irreg. 3rd Var.
O. Cromwell	13/7/1598 OS	20:55	3rd; Sex, Irreg. 1st Var.
Louis XIV	17/11/1637 NS	22:26:08	2nd; Sex, Irreg. 3rd Var.
T. Roosevelt	29/1/1858 NS	04:11:50	4th; Sex, Regular

Name	Birth Date	Birth Time	Birth Place
Cicero	3/1/106 BC	06:50:24	Arpino, Italy
Nero	15/12/37 AD	04:34:56	Anzio, Italy
Domitian	24/10/51AD	20:13:20	Rome, Italy
Henry VIII	28/06/1491OS	06:41:28	Greenwich, England
Philip II (E)	21/05/1527 OS	15:39:24	Valladolid, Spain
Elizabeth I	07/09/1533 OS	15:31:44	Greenwich, England
O. Cromwell	25/4/1599 OS	04:12:48	Huntingdon, England
Louis XIV	5/9/1638 NS	11:50:36	St. Germain-en-Laye, (F)
T. Roosevelt	27/10/1858 NS	12:04:12	New York, NY, USA

8)   Sign Decanate Distribution among the Three Main Chart Indicators:

Table 4:   Sign Decanate Distribution among the Nine, 2nd Tier, Power Notables.

Name	Sun	Moon	MoPo	Sun	Moon	MoPo
Cicero	3rd Pisces	3rd Capricorn	2nd Leo	2nd Capricorn	2nd Leo	3rd Capricorn
Nero	1st Pisces	1st Sagittarius	1st Pisces	3rd Sagittarius	1st Virgo	1st Sagittarius
Domitian	2nd Aquarius	1st Gemini	1st Sagittarius	1st Scorpio	1st Sagittarius	1st Gemini
Henry VIII	1st Libra	3rd Capricorn	1st Aries	2nd Cancer	1st Aries	3rd Cancer
Philip II	2nd Virgo	1st Taurus	3rd Leo	1st Gemini	3rd Aquarius	1st Scorpio
Elizabeth I	2nd Capricorn	3rd Aquarius	1st Taurus	3rd Virgo	1st Taurus	3rd Aquarius
O. Cromwell	1st Leo	2nd Aries	2nd Pisces	2nd Taurus	2nd Virgo	2nd Aries
Louis XIV	3rd Scorpio	2nd Sagittarius	1st Leo	2nd Virgo	1st Leo	2nd Sagittarius
T. Roosevelt	1st Aquarius	1st Leo	2nd Capricorn	1st Scorpio	2nd Cancer	1st Aquarius

The data in Table 4 show that although the 1st decanate of Scorpio features strongly it does not appear as often, relatively, as it does in

Table 1. In fact, here, the 1st decanates of Leo and Sagittarius appear more frequently. Other decanates that show as well as the 1st Scorpio decanate include the 1st decanates of Taurus and Gemini, the 2nd decanate of Virgo and the 3rd of Aquarius. Several decanates don't appear at all.. It is just worth mentioning that the charts of the only female power notable, QE1, show two 1st decanates of Taurus (due to the Order of the Epoch) that is directly opposite to the 1st decanate of Scorpio that appears to be important for male power notables.

See Appendix 3 for chapters on Cicero, Nero and Domitian, which we can compare with the previous power notable chapters. Extended Person Summaries have also been prepared for the other six, 2nd tier, power notables but without biographical extracts. However, they all fit well for the individual notable under consideration.

9) Overall Planetary Shaping:

Table 5: Overall Planetary Shaping of the Epoch and Birth Charts for the Nine, 2nd-Tier, Power Notables.

Name	Epoch Chart Shaping	Birth Chart Shaping
Cicero	Bucket (Mars handle)	Bucket (Moon handle)
Nero	Bucket (Mars handle)	Splay/Bowl
Domitian	Bundle + Moon singleton	Bundle + Mars singleton
Henry VIII	Bucket (Jupiter & Chiron handles)	Splash/See-Saw
Philip II	Bucket (Pluto handle)	Distorted bucket (Mars handle)
Elizabeth I	Distorted bucket (Saturn/Uranus handle)	Bucket (Jupiter & Pluto handles)
O. Cromwell	Bowl	Bowl
Louis XIV	Bundle (Pluto & Chiron handles?)	Bucket (Pluto & Chiron handles?)
T. Roosevelt	Bucket (Mars handle)	Splash

Table 5 shows that the most common shaping is the bucket just like the data in Chapter 7, Table 2. OC's charts are both closely related bowls and the shaping of Domitian's charts could easily be considered to be closely related to buckets. It would seem that the bucket shaping is the most relevant one for power notables.

10) Special Interplanetary Aspect Patterns:

Table 6: Special Interplanetary Aspect Patterns in the Charts of the Nine, 2nd-Tier, Power Notables.

Name	Epoch Chart	Birth Chart
Cicero	Distorted Grand Cross kite (Mars focus)	Capricorn Stellium. Sun BQ Jupiter and Neptune
Nero	Grand Trine Kite	--
Domitian	--	Grand Trine Kite
Henry VIII	Cardinal/Fixed Grand Cross	Fixed and Mutable T-Squares
Philip II	Mutable T-Square	Yod
Elizabeth I	--	--
O. Cromwell	--	Cardinal T-Square
Louis XIV	--	Fixed T-Square
T. Roosevelt	Fixed Grand Cross	Mutable T-Square + Fixed Grand Cross

Table 6 shows that apart from QEI (and Alexander the Great) all the power notables had some sort of strain aspect pattern. However, the occurrence of kites is not so striking, although Cicero, Nero, Domitian, KHVIII and particularly TR, all showed kites in their charts.

11) General Observations for the 2nd-Tier Power Notables: Only OC would have been expected to have a really lucky journey through life although Cicero, Domitian, KPII and KHVIII were also favoured. TR (like Alexander) succeeded despite relying too much on luck but Nero, QEI and KLXIV were not favoured. Apart from Domitian and KPII (and their situation was not that well-supported!) all the others would have met trouble dealing with the opposite sex.

12) Biographical Similarities: OC, QEI and TR in particular, but also Cicero, had to establish themselves during times of crisis. OC rose the most, followed by TR and then Cicero but all the others were born with silver spoons in their mouths. All were well educated. In terms of scale Nero probably achieved the least but the others all contributed significantly to society's development. KLXIV lived and

ruled by far the longest. Probably OC was responsible for the most deaths. Of these nine power notables TR was the one possessing most of the qualities of the first six but he was strongly influenced by Chiron and trusted to luck too much. QEI ruled/survived for 35 years, in what was definitely a man's world, by clever pragmatism, with the help of intelligent, trusted advisors and by personal charisma – all leading to popular consent. She provides us with a good example of a female power notable.

Implications

1) Combined interpretations of Epoch and Birth charts should become a more valuable guide for parents following the natural birth of any child. We could extend this to all horoscope interpretations.

2) Combined interpretations would form the basis for Person Summaries and Synastry Operations for Family History purposes and for potential romantic attachments, rather than interpretation of either the Epoch or Birth chart alone.

3) Techniques of Prediction should start from either or both of the Epoch and Birth charts, using each as the radix, as suggested by Bailey[1].

4) If it is true that we derive our characteristics from our genes (that consist entirely of DNA, and that have been well and truly established at our moment of fertilisation), then how is it that the Birth chart allows us to describe our characteristics (as it certainly seems to)? Furthermore, why is it that the Epoch chart, in itself, is not sufficient for this purpose?

5a) Topically, if we accept that the Moon plays an essential role in our birth on Earth, then we need to ask if human beings can survive for any protracted length of time away from the Earth/Moon/Sun system. If human life has to be confined to the Earth then we need to make sure that we secure the Earth's future, firstly by conserving its resources and environment and secondly by regulating population growth. Teilhard de Chardin describes evolution as driving towards increased consciousness. However, it carries this out without intelligence until it can continue no further. This blind groping towards increased consciousness could easily lead to the Earth becoming swamped by humans. Clearly we may well need to use our intelligence to control Earth's population growth to make life acceptable for us all. Probably this is far easier said than done!

5b) Is the human brain the most advanced organ for receiving and expressing abstract qualities?

5c) What influence do these Astrological findings have on an up-to-date ideology for our human situation?

Is it possible that, "Life on Earth is the only Flower in the Entire Universe"?

What's next?

This book has tried to show that Astrology can truthfully describe human characteristics. Assuming that this has been successful then the next step consists of proving the theory of "The Pre-Natal Epoch", one way or another, scientifically. The problem we have to solve comprises the accurate, independent determination of our Moment of Fertilisation (Pre-Natal Epoch) and then relate this to our accurate Moment of Birth. To achieve this, probably we should need first to study the birth process in large mammals more closely. Once we have confidently developed good techniques for doing so and have seen that a Pre-Natal Epoch theory for each mammal appears to work well, we can then try to extend the studies to our own birth process. In this way we can decide, once and for all, the Truth of Natal Astrology. However, this will be, perhaps, someone else's story . . . .

"Although we are Earthlings first, we are also, more importantly, Members of the Solar System."

- - - - - - - -- -

APPENDIX 1a

Indicators and Their Interpretations for the Epoch Chart of King Edward III.

Indicator	Interpretation
1) Chiron at handle of bucket shaping, slightly anticlockwise from centre[8].	Uncompromising direction to the life effort. Although not perfect himself he had a somewhat conservative approach to friends who tended to be both practical and critical[8].
2) Special Interplanetary Aspect Patterns	Not applicable.
3) Sun in Aquarius and Moon in Taurus[2].	True insight into human nature. Faithful, sincere, just and reliable. Robust and courageous manner. Good for friends, acquaintances, social and public relations generally[2].
4) Sun in 4th and Moon in 7th[3].	His strong family ties will make it difficult to transfer his attention to other people in society. He could not function well unless he was involved with people and most of his opportunities came from the social contacts he made. However, he wasn't sure that he could live up to their expectations of him. His first task was to become more detached from his family, putting them in the proper perspective that allowed him the independence to come and go as the demands of his career and social life required. His frame of reference had to be increasingly intellectual, not

	emotional, to improve his ability to solve the many problems that developed[3]. His ability to perform would have been increased if he could have avoided getting too deeply involved with the people he dealt with. Being emotionally committed in his duties would have severely limited his effectiveness. He should have postponed marrying until he was sure that he wasn't trying to compensate for a poor parental image in his choice of partner for such a situation is rarely satisfactory. Probably he would have enjoyed indulging his children; he had a strong mothering influence, and this may have satisfied his hunger for attention[3].
5a) Sun quintile Jupiter. 11th to 6th[4].	Cheerful and contented with his own surroundings. Opportunities expected and good luck[4]. He looked forward to the time when he could feel free of daily harassment and effort. By using all his resources he could easily have achieved that goal[3]
5b) Moon conjoint Mars, 1st to 7th; opposition Neptune, 7th to 7th;	Robust, courageous manner, though over-active at times and over-quick in response[4]. His need for companionship meant that he had to make many concessions to others. Generally, he waited for the other person to make the first move because he feared rejection or lack of interest[3]. Enhanced sensitivity but also **deceit and gullibility possible**[4]. He needed to resist the urge to marry the first likely prospect. His early training led him to believe that it was better to marry anyone than to remain single. With that attitude he could have ended up being single again. A strong mothering

sextile Venus, 3rd to 5th, Sesquiquadrate Saturn.	urge was always in the background of his consciousness[3]. Simply, he wanted people to like him[3]. There was happiness in domestic conditions but relations with women and mother were not easy[4].
6) Scorpio contains the Morin Point[5] in its first decanate[6].	**At its worst he had a criminal personality seeking fulfilment of personal aims without regard for the feelings of others. However if these tendencies can be resisted, honest success can be achieved by means of a thrusting, purposeful nature, and a capacity for hard work[5].** Prudent, self-controlled, highly dignified[6].
7) Ruler Pluto in Pisces in 5th[7], square Uranus 4th to 2nd[3], and sextile Saturn 3rd to 3rd[3].	**Compassion and imagination stimulated.** Renunciation becomes an obsession with a compelling need to achieve understanding[7]. He knew what he wanted and how to get it. If necessary he would flatter people when he wanted to win them over. He was concerned about social problems and had many ideas to solve them[3]. It annoyed him to be without money but he had no excuse because his creative talents should have allowed him to increase your resources. He expected more for his efforts than he deserved because he didn't want to give up his indulgences. He should have applied himself[3].
8) No rising planet.	Not applicable
9) Mercury trine Chiron, 5th to 11th.	He was well-liked by his friends because he didn't threaten their egos. There was never a dull moment when he was around for he lent sparkle and wit to any gathering. He gave and accepted help from close friends[3].

APPENDIX 1b

Indicators and Their Interpretations for the Birth Chart of

King Edward III.

Indicator	Interpretation
1) Eastern emphasis. See-Saw shaping. Fanhandle[8].	*Destiny in his own hands[12].* *Tendency to act at all times under a consideration of opposing views or through a sensitiveness to contrasting and antagonistic possibilities. Capable of unique achievement through a development of unsuspected relations in life but also apt to waste his energies through being out-of-touch with prevailing conditions[8].*
2) Retrograde Jupiter, in Taurus in 7th, malasp., focal planet of fanhandle pattern. Retrograde in Taurus. Retrograde in 7th.	*Over-exaggerated desire to aggrandise himself through more land and what this can achieve. Not so fortunate in marriage or with good management relations[4].* *He was often overly impressed with his competitors' qualifications as he was less forceful than he should have been in asserting himself and his talents. If someone he loved and respected had a strong belief in his abilities he would listen to them[3].* *He concentrated much energy establishing that he was always right. This made it difficult for him to adapt himself to other people's way of thinking. He stubbornly held on to past concepts (e.g. belief in moribund trades such as tinker, cobbler, gourmet-chef or bookbinder). His ego problem related to unrealistic expectations from life. He needed to feel dominant but learnt his greatest truths in the most natural way and only at times when he was not trying to impress others or exert himself[11].*

Opposition Neptune.	*He looked at himself as seen through the eyes of others. He experienced impatience trying to please others. He taught himself to stand for what he thought others would admire. He would argue to uphold a principle rather than for his own need to win. He could become overly self-righteous and needed to learn that differences between right and wrong lay strictly in the mind of each individual. He was learning to balance the nature of truth through the many ways it was expressed from person to person in his life[11].* *Treachery, **deceit and gullibility**[4].*
3) Sun in Scorpio and Moon in Taurus.	*Positiveness softened but with increased display and management success. He was firm and determined. He had a fixed course of life and persisted and persevered to carry it out. He lived in a grove all his life. His domestic and social sides were well-developed. Music and art were cultivated. Cheerful and generally good-natured. Fairly fortunate through life[2].*
4) Sun in 1st and Moon in 7th[3].	*It is in response to the challenges and competition presented by others that he eventually proved himself. Challenge was the most stimulating condition for him and he literally glowed as he rose to the occasion. When situations bogged him down and he got bored and lost interest, he thrived on the many confrontations that he faced. It disturbed him to be ignored as he was much more sensitive than others realised. He was completely involved with the world around him; his ultimate ambition being to gain full control over his circumstances. He made certain concessions in order to win others' support in his climb to prominence. He had self-determination and the leverage of power. Education*

	supported his purposes, leading to involvement with large numbers of people from a position of authority[3]. He had difficulty gaining the independence he needed from family obligations but he used his charm to avoid alienation. He needed to be involved in a partnership so marriage was an asset to him in his future plans. His mate must have been willing to share his enthusiasm for what he hoped to accomplish, which would have improved the quality of life for his family[3].
5a) Moon trine Saturn, 6th to 2nd. 5b) Only weak aspects to the Sun but sextile Chiron, 3rd to 11th.	Willing acceptance of duty and success through orderly and practical ways, even though these may cause personal limitations and lack of gaiety[4]. He would have become interested in occupations that brought him before the public. His sensitive understanding of human problems proved an asset for public service but he had to be careful not to allow people to use him as a doormat[3]. He could win friends and influence people through his charm. He knew that careful planning was the best way to achieve his goals[3].
6) Scorpio contains the Morin Point[5] in its 3rd decanate.Mars, Venus, Neptune, Sun and Uranus all in 1st, Stellium[12]	*At his worst a criminal personality seeking fulfilment of personal aims without the regard for the feelings of others. However when these tendencies were resisted, honest success could be achieved by means of a thrusting, purposeful nature and a capacity for hard work[5].* There was a keen desire for attachment that tended to counter selfishness. However, jealous tendencies were exacerbated[6].
7) Ruler Pluto in Pisces in 4th,	*Compassion and imagination stimulated. Becomes obsessed with renunciation with a compelling need to*

square Uranus.	*achieve understanding. Great transformations inherited. Isolated circumstances at the end of life. Vital and deeply upsetting parental influence. Restless in birthplace – whole world his home[7].*
	Self-willed, fanatical, eccentric, can read character, explosive, physical strength, nervous disorders. Tendency to be dogmatic, rashness, quarrelling, boasting, inner struggles. Father dies young[7].
4th to 1st.	*Alienating circumstances in his home forced him to assert himself and feel confident so that he was able to succeed on his own[3].*
8) Rising planets: Mars, Venus, Neptune, 7th to 7th; Sun.	*His greatest danger was being deceived by others. He should have had to check everyone's credentials and he had to believe only the facts that checked out. He should have had legal advice even for insignificant contracts[3].*
Venus conjoint Mars.	*He had ability to love, to enjoy sexual life and all things of beauty were strengthened and made more robust but less delicate[4].*
1st to 1st, Venus.	***He was genial, warm and affectionate** He always tried to be pleasant because he truly enjoyed people. He won the approval of those around him by conceding to their desires if he could[3].*
1st to 1st, Mars.	*He was restless and eager and when stimulated his aggressive nature sprang into action. It was the thrill of competition that made him accept challenges. He thrived on sensationalism and conflict[3].*
9) Mercury in Sagittarius in 2nd.	*Mentality not well-integrated with the rest of the personality. Thoughts expressed in "far-flung", decisive, money-making ways not necessarily a part of his true character; they needed to be guarded against[4].*
Unaspected.	*He was immediately aware when anyone tried to*
Pentaundecile	*undermine him or resorted to unjust practices. He was*

Jupiter, 8th to 7th.	*willing to make sacrifices for the "right" person, with whom he hoped to share his life, and no gift was too costly when he wanted to impress that person[3].*

APPENDIX 2a

Indicators and Their Interpretations for the Epoch Chart of

Adolf Hitler

Indicator	Interpretation
1) Neptune conjoint Pluto in Gemini in 6th[3], leads bowl shaping[8].	Tendency to capture things. Has a self-containment because he is set-off against a segment of experience from which he is excluded. Unoccupied segment becomes a challenge to existence. He has something to give to his fellows either constructively or vindictively. An idealist, who advocates some cause, furtherance of a mission, an introspective concern over the purpose of existence[8].
2) Mutable/Fixed T-square. Venus is focus in Virgo in 9th, Malasp.	Tends to adjust to, or to by-pass, or to put up with difficulties but not without nervous strain[4]. Fond of study, of intelligent interests and of travel but disappointment in these. He allowed his critical facility and his constant fuss about detail to interfere with the harmony of his life[4].
3) Sun in Leo and Moon in Scorpio[2]	Austerity given with an inclination to be rather hard, proud and arrogant. There is much love of show. Bright, creative nature can be quite hidden under the hard exterior. Attracted by the senses (mental in this case). In love affairs, or where sensation is concerned there is a danger of going to excesses and this should be guarded against for a reckless or careless life could damage the heart. Not fortunate for mother or wife; there is liability to separate from, or death of one of them. Very fixed and

	determined nature, ardent but at times too positive, worldly and sensual. He would have made a good, magnetic healer[2].
4) Sun in 8th and Moon in 11th[3].	As he was delayed in getting his career underway, it was probably because he couldn't decide which field would give him the greatest return for his efforts. He was deeply preoccupied with finding a job that would give him security in his later years, rather than one that permitted him to exploit his creative talents as fully as possible. Perhaps he should have backed up a little and re-examined his motivations. He may have discovered that his creative potential could have satisfied certain needs of the larger society. He was offered many opportunities for applying his skills where they were most urgently needed. When he focused on providing a service that made demands on his creative talent, security for the future was a natural bi-product[3]. Communications, government service, politics, social service, vocational guidance and teaching were some of the ways to use his talent and make a worthwhile contribution to society. Nothing was as satisfying as knowing that he had helped make the world a better place for everyone. If he and his partner had complemented each other, both of them would have been supported in reaching their goals[3].
5a) No strong aspects to the Sun. 5b) Moon trine Chiron, 5th to 7th[3].	Finds helpful, protective support from others within societies and groups. He worked very hard to convince his partner that he cared when probably it wasn't necessary. His partner already gave him all the support he needed to expand his area of responsibility[3].

6) Morin Point in Capricorn[5], 1st Decanate[6]. Saturn above the Earth but starting to set. Uranus in 10th in Libra.	A persistent, self-controlled personality capable of achieving success through hard work. Practical abilities are usually combined with a shrewd mind and inner stability[5]. Increased ambition. Misfortunes and obstacles tend to beset the path[6]. Harmonious impulses awakened. Aesthetic appreciation. Co-operative; spirit of compromise, power of judgement; self-adjustment. Rigidity destroyed, fitful will, fickle. A splendid leader in the affairs of the world with vision and readiness to change old ways. Awkward if not in a position to lead[7].
7) Ruler Saturn in Leo in 8th; conjoint Mercury, square Mars.

1st to 8th[3]. | Limitation is on power to express self in creative, happy ways. Enjoyment of life did not come easily[4]. Responsibility through affairs of others either through personal cares or through losses caused by them. Seriousness over sexual affairs. Careful interest in psychic matters and thoughts about death and about the after-life develop when older[4]. Mental and nervous powers will be limited and dullness results. Through apprehension prudence will be increased. Depression may be frequent. Strained energy will result in a mind without width but with great power of concentration and drive[4]. He tried to avoid being obliged to others, although his circumstances indicated that he could not really expect it. He compared his resources with those of others as though he thought his self-worth should be determined only by his personal and material assets. A patient working out of what is begun but not with ease. Results must be battled for. Nervousness |

131

10th to 11th.	engendered produces selfishness and egocentricity. Hardness is endured and sternness given. Danger of accidents by burns, scalds and falling. Physical overstrain is risked[4]. Only a career with a future interested him. He was best suited to working with the public, which would have allowed him to expand his range of influence as his skills improved[3].
8) No rising planets, etc.	Not applicable

APPENDIX 2b

Indicators and Their Interpretations for the Birth Chart of

Adolf Hitler.

Indicator	Interpretation
1) Splay Shaping. Western and Southern emphasis.	*Highly individual or purposeful emphases in the life, where the temperament juts out into experience according to its own very special tastes. Robust resistance to pigeon-holing. Awkward certainty to every approach he made to problems of life. Intensive personality who cannot be limited to any steady point of application. A temperament that is particular but at the same time impersonal[18].* *Overall fate is in the hands of others, or circumstances[12]. Objective rather than subjective[12].*
2) Quintile family kite.	*Stressed but intelligent personality. Principles of planets involved are well-integrated within his personality[4].*
3) Sun in Taurus and Moon in Capricorn.	*Practical (able to build-up a fortune), careful and cautious with an aptitude for making very carefully thought-out plans and schemes that generally are carried out successfully. Very independent, determined and highly ambitious but chiefly concerned with conventional ideals pertaining to physical objects and personal surroundings. Especially adapted for public life. Ability to deal with big schemes; to organise and carry-out huge plans. Good vitality and long life[2].*
4) Sun in 7th and Moon in 3rd.	*His ability to succeed was enhanced by the ease with which he got involved with people. He enjoyed being in the mainstream of human activity and he had a talent for*

	getting people to support him in his enterprises. He was generally eager to reciprocate when others needed his help, which benefitted him in his long-range goals. He knew how to use opportunities that came through others to achieve the greatest yield, sometimes exceeding the rewards enjoyed by those who made the opportunities available. People sought his advice on important matters because he had such good insight, so a career requiring this kind of talent would have been a good choice[3].
	A career that allowed him self-determination would have given him a say about his growth and progress in his field. A routine job was not for him because it would have denied him the full development of his rich, creative potential. Journalism, writing, broadcasting, any of the communications media, law, politics or government service were appropriate for his talent and temperament[3].
	Probably he would have formed a permanent relationship fairly early on in life. If his partner had been equally fascinated with change and progress, he would have been very happy. Because he rarely looked back his future rewards were limited only by the commitment he was willing to make to them[3].
5a) Sun exactly semisextile Neptune. 12th to 8th.	*Attracted to music, art, dancing, psychism and mysticism. A tendency to all matters to do with the sea[4]. He underestimated his ability to make an important contribution to society. He was sensitive to human frailty and knew how to solve the problems it caused. He might have married for financial gain or simply because he didn't like living alone, which were not the best reasons. It would have been better to marry because he felt he had met his ideal mate[3].*
5b) Moon	*Optimism, good health and a tendency to a lucky journey*

conjoint Jupiter, 1st to 3rd.	*through life[4].* *He was naturally inquisitive especially about his immediate environment and family. His mind was retentive and he rarely forgot anything he learnt. However, his emotional bias made it difficult for him to separate fact from fiction sometimes[3].*
6) Morin Point in 1st Scorpio decanate. Sun has set.	*At his worst a criminal personality seeking fulfilment of personal aims without regard for the feelings of others. However, if these tendencies can be resisted, honest success can be achieved by means of a thrusting, purposeful nature and a capacity for hard work[5].* *Fate could be tragic and unfortunate[6].*
7) Ruler Pluto in 8th in Gemini. Pluto exact sesquiquadrate Uranus, 9th to 12th.	*Stimulated sensation seeking. Inventiveness. Search for novelty. Impetuosity. Obsession is mobility with a compelling need to achieve comprehension (too clever?). Vital search for the meaning of life. Death in public place, unfortunate end. Greatly concerned over monetary resources[7].* *Stimulated will. Highly independent. Determined (fanatical), could read character (eccentric, perverted), spiritual energy, physical strength, and endurance[7].* *His sensitivity to unacceptable social conditions may have forced him to make some sacrifices to ensure the elimination of these conditions. Many legal resources were available to help him force the public to re-examine the social values involved[3].*
8) No rising planets but Venus retrograde in Taurus in 7th.	*Shy earlier, he wanted others to bring him out. Tried to draw others to him quietly but finally the world passed him by. Unrealistic expectations of the opposite sex owing to powerful self-delusion he had been holding for many years. Silently collected one chip on his shoulder after another, after another . . . His feelings were like a*

Venus exact conjunction Mars. 1st to 7th.	*pendulum swinging from side to side by the winds of other people's feelings, always passing the centre but never staying there. He was never quite sure that he was seen as proper in the eyes of others. Highly sensitive to his external environment he experienced the unbalanced parts of himself through the ways in which others saw him[11].* *His ability to love and enjoy sexual life and all things of beauty was strengthened and made more robust but less delicate[4].* *His conciliatory manner endeared him to those with whom he was in close personal contact. He always seemed to make concessions especially when a situation developed that could cause disharmony between himself and others[3].*

136

APPENDIX 3

Marcus Tullius Cicero

"Cedant arma togae"
"The military should yield to the Government"

Cicero was a Roman philosopher, constitutionalist, statesman, lawyer and political theorist. He came from a wealthy family of the equestrian order (knight) and is widely considered one of Rome's greatest orators and prose stylists. He introduced the Romans to the main schools of Greek philosophy and created a Latin philosophical vocabulary.

Cicero probably thought that his political career was his most important achievement but today he is appreciated primarily for his humanism, together with his philosophical and political writings. His voluminous correspondence, much of it to his friend Atticus, introduced the art of refined letter writing to European culture. The wealth of detail in his letters about the inclinations of leading men, the faults of generals and the revolutions of the government left readers with little need for a history of the 1st century BC.

During the civil wars and Caesar's resulting dictatorship, Cicero supported a return to republican government. However, he tended to shift his position in response to change in the political climate. His indecision and over-reaction in the face of political and private change can be attributed to his sensitive and impressionable personality. Asinius Pollio, a contemporary Roman statesman and historian said, "Would that he had been able to endure prosperity with greater self-control and adversity with fortitude."

M. T. Cicero – Horoscopes

Cicero was born on the 3rd January, 106 BC about 7 a.m. at Arpino, Italy. His father was Marcus and his mother, Helvia. The more likely of his two possible Epochs* occurred on the 21st March, 107 BC just before 3 p.m. (see Figure 13). The chart shaping is a "bucket" with Mars as the vertical handle and the Jupiter – Sun opposition as the bucket rim. This shaping gives a particular and uncompromising direction to his life-effort (towards personal fame) within which the Mars handle provides him with the capacity to shift his interests[3]. Mars in Gemini in the 11th House (just) suggests that he would have been energetically talkative with constant change of direction. He would have been quick to make friends but would have lost them easily by being too pushy and quarrelsome. Jupiter in Virgo in the 3rd House, opposition to the Sun conjoint Neptune in Pisces in the 9th House, gave him extraordinary sensitivity combined with an enlarged capacity for communication. The mutable T-square of the handle and bucket rim (note that Mars, again, is the focal planet here) becomes converted into a weak Grand-Cross (a particular sort of kite) by the opposition of Mars to Uranus. This means that he will

----

*At Cicero's birth the Moon was above the Earth (Morin Point) and decreasing in light so that his Epoch was 2nd Order. According to Bailey's Table of Sex Degrees the Moon at birth occupied a male position and the corresponding Morin Point lay in a female one, making the Epoch a Sex one. For this case there are two valid, likely Epochs. One occurs on the 3rd April, 107 BC, just after 2 p.m. and the second on the 21st March, 107 BC, just before 3 p.m. Examination of the aspects received by the Sun and Moon for both Epochs strongly suggests that the 2nd, earlier Epoch, fits Cicero better, bearing in mind his renowned sensitivity. As a result this Epoch was chosen for Cicero.

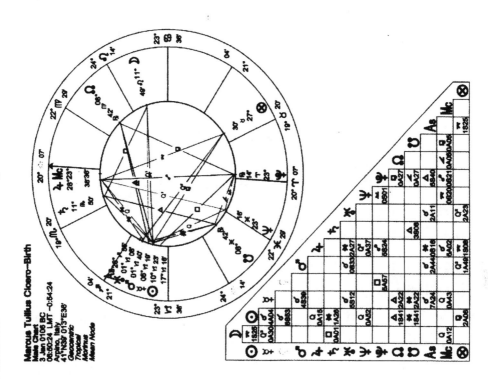

Figure 14: Birth Chart and Aspect Grid for M. T. Cicero.

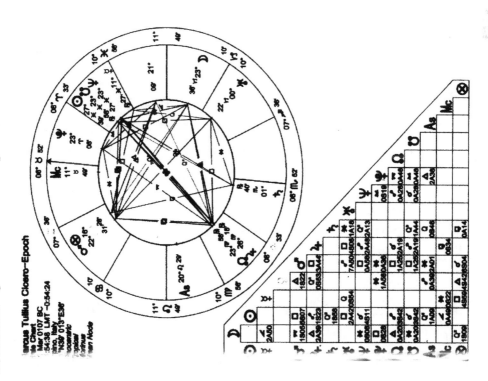

Figure 13: Epoch Chart and Aspect Grid for M. T. Cicero.

139

try to adjust to difficulties and try to by-pass them but not without nervous strain. The Sun – Moon polarity of Pisces and Capricorn respectively means that he tended to be practical rather than dreamy and one for whom an active life was best. The Sun in the 9th House – Moon in the 6th House polarity means that he had to resign himself to working to achieve his goals. The strong aspects of both the Sun and Moon to both Neptune and Jupiter not only emphasised his sensitivity but also his good luck and his store of creative ideas. The Morin Point in Leo provided him with a love of power, organising ability and good vitality. Jupiter in Virgo in the 3rd House is his 2nd decanate ruler and as it is poorly aspected in general (opposition to the Sun), it points to his exaggerated habit of constant criticism from his inflated spiritual ego. This Epoch generates the Ideal Birth chart and aspect grid shown in Figure 14. Together these charts contain eight quintile family aspects indicating Cicero's high intelligence. Once again the overall shaping is a "bucket" with the singleton Moon in Leo in the 8th House as the somewhat anticlockwise handle to the Jupiter – Pluto rim.   This confirms the particular and uncompromising direction to Cicero's life-effort and gives him a conservative leaning when dealing with public affairs. The Stellium (5 planets) in Capricorn emphasises his practical, cautious, responsible and ambitious side. The Sun in Capricorn – Moon in Leo polarity means that his affections tended to conflict with his internal ambitions and the Sun in the 1st House – Moon in the 8th House meant that he needed to make sacrifices during his drive for achievement. Notice that the Sun is bi-quintile to Jupiter and to Neptune suggesting his need for self-determination supported by his creative ideas. The Sun is also sextile to Saturn (ruler) showing his good acceptance of his limitations but as the Moon is exactly square to Saturn then he would have met difficulties with his mother and with women in general. The Morin Point in Capricorn supports his persistent and persevering disposition while the ruler (Saturn) in

Scorpio in the 11th House shows that caution and limitation were expressed with reserve and secrecy. Elderly or serious friends would have been the most satisfying for him. Venus rising in Capricorn favours him socially and indicates that he was devoted when attached. The Sun rising in Capricorn gives him an illustrious, moral and self-controlled look. As explained previously, note that Chiron is absent from both charts but also that there is no strong Scorpio influence in either of them.

Person Summary with Biographical Extracts

Character

General: There appear to have been two, main, opposing sides to Cicero's nature, each influenced by a third. For the first main part he was practical rather than dreamy, cautious, responsible, persevering and even plodding, yet anxious to be at the head of affairs. 'He had an unquenchable, but non-military, thirst for personal fame. Although he hated war, when young, he had to serve in the army of Strabo, where he met Pompey, during the War of the Allies. This experience probably served him well when he became Governor of Cilicia, which he defended successfully against the Parthians, who had recently defeated and killed Crassus at the battle of Carrhae.' He was inclined to become a utilitarian and to serve others. This first main part was set off against an optimistic, fearless, self-reliant, frank, moral, generous, kindly, honourable and even illustrious part, ambitious for power and distinction. As a result, an active life was best for him and, provided that he worked hard without concern to preserve himself or his resources, then he could accept responsibility and take the lead. He tended to win through despite all obstacles. 'In Homer's Iliad, Glaucus says to Diomedes "Always be the best, my boy, the bravest, and hold your head high above the others." This quotation had also inspired Alexander the Great.' He depended

141

a little too much on luck and there was a conceited, imprudent and extravagant aspect to his character with a dramatic love of ostentation, exaggeration and display. Yet he did have a tendency to a lucky journey through life meeting good opportunities and helpful people. Thirdly, he could also be self-willed, insistent, awkward, brusque and even revolutionary. Moreover, there was an attraction for musical and artistic accomplishment, to dancing, spiritualism and to all matters to do with the sea (apart from sailing on it!)

<u>Mentality:</u>   Mentally active, extremely sensitive and energetically talkative (he had an inability to hold his tongue, was over confident when things went well yet setbacks drove him into an exaggerated depression) he was keen on any idea or objective. With his mental and intellectual strength, backed-up by a good education, he proved a useful and important member of society. His ideals were high regarding his surroundings, whether artistic, social or political. He would have had an interest in sexual matters (his correspondence with Caerullia was risqué), in psychic research and in speculation about the after-life. Highly imaginative, he was a whirlwind of ideas, and with only a little help he could have used these ideas to obtain his basic necessities. Much could have been given out following the reception of ideas and influences. There was no doubt that he had a strong tendency to the intangible and the abstract with a resulting lack of concreteness. All his prudence, forethought, quietness, sobriety and self-control was accompanied by gloom, despondency and a concomitant lack of initiative. 'He lost weight and cried a lot when he was expelled from Rome.'

His mind could show confusion and desperation in that he needed to know the questions before he could discover the answers. He had trouble separating his mental energies from his intuition. He thought that others did not understand the scope of his ideas and that language was rather inadequate to express them so that, literally, he thought that he lost the essence of his ideas. There was conflict between joining the world as he saw it and desiring to escape it. He wondered if the values of social acceptance represented any reality at all. Thus there was poor opportunity for expressing his imagination and creative originality. On the one hand he could say much in a few words but, on the other, tended to scatter his mental energies yet judged others adversely for doing the same thing. In some ways he showed a lack of perspective (he tended to lack Caesar's clarity of vision). He lifted himself into higher levels of consciousness. He was an unusually deep thinker whose thought processes went right to the heart of life's essential meanings. 'He showed phenomenal productivity as a writer.' He manipulated himself into the construction of unrealistic belief systems (e.g. his belief in a mixed constitution), which he tried to live up to. He may have experienced sexual problems because the depth of his thinking made him question constantly the value of all physical expression. He tended to trap himself, fighting his needs, and so isolated himself from the realities of his existence. He never accepted a superficial answer to his questions but sought to know the ultimate why of all that exists. Sometimes he thought that he was alienated from society and so could have become a product of destructive thoughts but he could also generate constructive action to carry out in the present. He was a regenerator of human thought but he needed to listen carefully to the words of advice he gave to others because these very words would have turned out to be his own guidance for himself. Contentment finally came when he stopped trying to be a symbol for all he thought mankind expected of itself.

Lifestyle: The limitation to his self-expression (e.g. his nervousness, difficulties with women and his fear of physical aggression), which he had become conditioned to, had been well-accepted. Wisdom, patience and constructiveness grew and brought success in later life. 'As Cicero's life developed he became less volatile, meeting challenges and misfortunes with determination. Caution was expressed as strong reserve and limitations were kept secret. He used his capacity to shift his interests well because he was subject to upsets and forced new phases. At times, explosive himself, he was likely to end conditions (his sudden divorce of Terentia after more than thirty years of marriage left an unpleasant taste) and force new beginnings but with good results after a painful crisis. He dug deeply into life and poured forth the result of his gathered experience with unremitting zeal. He met difficulties, limitations and frustrations since his very nature was conditioned to them, and he tried to adjust to, or to by-pass, them, although not without nervous stress, as already indicated.

Relationships

Others: Cicero admired people who had distinguished themselves through their achievements and he hoped to emulate them. Genial, warm and affectionate he always tried to be pleasant because he truly enjoyed people. He won the approval of those around him by conceding to their desires if he possibly could. He had a deep, spiritual devotion to people who were somehow disadvantaged (he defended Sicilians against Verres) so he tried to get the training he needed in order to serve them better, which was his social obligation. His knowledge sustained those who needed intellectual nourishment but he came to believe that he was superior to others spiritually because of the purity of his ideas. He tended to be abrupt with people liking to cover a great deal of ground in a short time and yet he himself would be overly talkative. Eventually it became impossible for people to live up to his expectations of them. 'After proscription, his severed head was taken to Fulvia, Mark Antony's wife, who pulled out the tongue and stabbed it repeatedly in a defiant gesture of revenge.'

<u>Friends:</u> Cicero's social life was favoured because he was attractive and desirable. 'His school friends admired him for his academic ability but also for his sense of humour.' He knew how to win friends and influence people with his charming manner and winning ways. He was quick to make friends but lost them by being overly pushy and quarrelsome. Elderly, serious friends were the most satisfying (e.g. Atticus and Sulpicius Rufus). Actually, there was a lack of real friendship, rather a concentration on objectives that may have become burdensome (his career was his overriding interest). However, in general, he could depend on friends when he needed them (with the possible exception of Pompey).

<u>Family:</u> If Cicero had waited for his parents' approval he would never have established his own goals. Probably he always had pleasant and advantageous relations with his siblings (but he tended to treat his younger brother, Quintus, as an extension of himself rather than as an independent figure in his own right). At some time in his life he had to make the commitment of using his gifts to enhance the quality of life for others, including his partner and his children. He expressed warmth to youngsters in his family (e.g. to his nephew, Quintus and particularly to his daughter, Tullia), who served as the best stimulant for the success he was to achieve. His driving desire to see his children rise to prominence could have blinded his ability to accept what they may choose to do with their lives if it differed from his expectations. 'There seemed to be some disappointment with his son, Marcus.'

<u>Lover:</u> Irresolute and fickle in affection early on, there was the tendency that Cicero's partnerships were subject to disclosures, upheavals and new starts with trouble and unpleasantness. His relations with his mother (despite his copious writings he never mentioned his mother) and with women in general, were not easy. His emotional side could have led to him becoming dangerously demoralised through passion and sensuality. Troublingly his

affections conflicted with his internal ambitions so that he tended to back away from intimate relations with others. This denial of relationships intensified his shyness and prevented easy response to what could have brought happiness. However, warmth and enthusiasm entered into his affections in sexual life. In fact, he prided himself on how well he could satisfy his partner's needs (e.g. those of his young, second wife, Publilia) and in relations he demanded the privilege of mobility for himself. But his deepest emotions were very single-minded and he became devoted when he was attached (to Terentia and Tullia). His partner should have helped him to relieve his anxiety about being useful to society. There was gain through marriage (Terentia brought a large dowry with her).

Career

Early: Fate would rule Cicero rather than his ability to decide his own destiny. His fate was affected by his moral growth, by his power to organise and by his ability to rise above the difficulties of his early environment. Success was indicated through all educational matters, writings and communication (he seems to have modelled his oratorical style on the actor, Q. Roscius Gallus). He was somewhat apprehensive about his future and about successfully reaching his goals. Probably he believed it was necessary to work as an apprentice to earn the career position he wanted but it was easier to work at getting an education and it would have saved him a great deal of time. As his learning ability and memory were better than most, all that he needed was the determination to acquire the skills needed for responsible positions. Actually, his progress was greatly simplified by getting an education but he had to learn to stand on his own before hoping to achieve accomplishments. With a little self-reliance and careful planning he could have achieved most of his objectives. However, he could not have afforded to become one of those who were content to be average in what they do (See Homer quote, earlier), so that the only way to distinguish himself was to reach a higher level of competence. Basically, he could have fulfilled his life's work through action, not words. By making a courageous effort to put his ideas to work he achieved a position (i.e. 1st Consul of the Roman republic) he wanted. That was the only way to get the recognition he deserved. All his dreams and desires of what he hoped to achieve were meaningless unless he was resigned to the necessity of working to achieve them. Some position of trust or responsibility advanced his cause and depending on his self-possession, tact and prudence he advanced, made successful progress gaining fame, recognition or honour. 'The legal case that made Cicero's reputation was that of Chrysogonus.' He was suited to a wide variety of service professions including law, medicine, social service, vocational guidance, unions, research and development, engineering, physical therapy and teaching aids. He had ability for occupations dealing with the public and was fitted for occupying a prominent position. He could have done so much to help relieve social problems that it would have been a significant loss to society and to himself, if he had neglected this task (i.e. his constitutional and philosophical writings). He had keen insight into people's problems and once he had been trained to deal with them he would have enjoyed comfortable earnings. But until he could offer the professional services that people needed he had to stay clear of friends and associates who wanted him to help them with their problems. It might have been flattering to his ego to indulge them, but eventually they would have abused the privilege.

<u>Middle:</u>   Although Cicero overvalued the practical and had a tendency to meet hardships, there were strong indications for success in life. He may not have been able to choose a professional career but he would have conducted himself professionally in his work. He knew the limits of his training and education but he also knew that

he could make a proper place for himself in the world and win recognition (he determined to excel in the Forum). He planned carefully because he knew that that was the best way to achieve his goals. Through experience he learned from those who failed as well as from those who succeeded and because he was never satisfied with his level of accomplishment he tried to get more from his efforts by improving his skills and by pursuing greater conquests. With inspiration, vision and imagination he was able to become the best in his field. His most urgent priority should have been to ask questions. He should never have assumed that he was well enough informed about any subject, for his continuing progress depended on his sustained interest and enthusiasm. There was a particular and uncompromising direction to his life-effort so that he adopted his allegiances to lines along which he could make his efforts count for the most. He wanted to become self-employed, if possible, but even if he had been employed by others he would have had to have self-determination in his job. This facet of his personality could have been a response to early parental intimidation that threatened his self-image. He was able to make it on his own but needed to be convinced of that fact. He wanted to be free to use his creativity in activities that were far removed from the usual, boring routine (such as dealing with abstract qualities). He could have earned a comfortable income from the products, services or professional expertise that he offered. He had to be guarded about revealing his ideas until they were sufficiently developed so he could apply them. He ran the risk of sharing too easily and having others appropriate his ideas for their benefit, excluding him from the rewards he sought. He hoped that someday he could prove how effective he was in serving the public's best interests and he must have had to work hard and to have extended himself to win the public's support. Because he was responsive to people's needs he was in a desirable position to win recognition for his efforts and he might well have chosen a career in public, rather than private, service. He channelled his energies into affairs that fulfilled other people's needs to relieve his anxiety about being useful to society and realised that unless he was willing to devote some part of his life to helping people to become more self-reliant his growth would be limited. He responded to matters dealing with legacies and contracts and there was gain through these (he made a fortune from legacies). He hoped that he was not being naïve when he offered to help others, assuming that he would have been repaid for his efforts when he least expected it. He was sensitive to an appeal for help, especially when it was a sincere request for assistance. As he asserted himself in his drive for achievement there were times when he had to make sacrifices. Some of these may have required him to indulge others in their needs, which he could have regarded as an investment in his own plans to reach his goals. Eventually he must have had to be involved in the affairs of society at large, e.g. in parliament, to feel that he had made any lasting contribution to solving its problems. A conflict with "The Powers That Be" was indicated. 'His aristocratic, natural allies, who controlled the Senate, were unwilling to welcome him into their ranks because they hated him as a "New Man". This was emotionally debilitating and embittering for him.'

<u>Late:</u> Cicero owed the public the benefit of his developing talents and skills and once he was established his growth was assured. With favourable conditions there was a very great power for good. His eventful life was the outcome of his love of power and his organising ability. Hasty and passionate impulses could have caused downfalls but he recovered through firmness, endurance and self-control. He had financial ability concerning property with the power to organise, arrange, manage, plan and scheme about it. 'As soon as he could afford it Cicero became a landlord and a property developer.'

Health

Cicero had good health (despite an early trip to Greece because of poor health) with a tendency to great vitality, good physique and a strong body. His nervous system was responsive. Accordingly he may have expected to live a long life but there was some likelihood of an accidental, or rather sudden, death. 'He was assassinated rather suddenly following unexpectedly unfortunate events leading to his proscription, '

Reference: "Cicero – A Turbulent Life", A. Everitt, J. Murray, Ltd., London, 2001.

- -

Nero

"Qualis artifex pereo"
"What an artist dies in me"

Nero ruled Rome from 54 – 68 AD focussing on diplomacy, trade and increasing the cultural capital of the empire. He ordered the building of theatres and promoted athletic games. His reign included the successful war and negotiated peace with the Parthian Empire (58-63), the suppression of the British revolt (60-61) and the start of the canal at the Isthmus of Corinth, Greece. The first Roman-Jewish  war began during his reign (66-70) but a military coup drove him from the throne. Fearing assassination he committed suicide in 68. His rule is associated with tyranny and extravagance. For example, he arranged the murder of both his mother and his 1st wife, probably his adoptive brother and persecuted the Christians. On the other hand, he built the "Domus Aurea" and was popular with the common Roman people, especially in the East, due to the good relations developed with Parthia.

Nero – Horoscopes

Nero was born* on the 15th December, 37 AD at 04:35 at Antium, Italy, the only son of 12 children to his father, Gnaeus Ahenobarbus, who died when Nero was 3, and to his mother, Agrippina the Younger, Caligula's sister. His Epoch* occurred on the 23rd February, 37 AD at

- -

* At Nero's birth the Moon was above the Earth and decreasing in light so his Epoch was 2nd Order. The Morin Point at birth occupied a male position and the Moon's position was neutral (negative). Thus his Epoch was Irregular, 2nd or 3rd Variation, both giving rise to a male birth

06:18. The Epoch chart (see Figure 15) shows a 'bucket' shaping having the Sun/Mercury conjunction opposite to the Uranus/Saturn conjunction as its rim with the North, singleton, anticlockwise, handle planet Mars in the 5th House in Gemini. Apart from a particular and rather uncompromising direction to his life-effort this suggests that he was energetically talkative and gaily enjoying love-making, children, games and all pleasures, harmlessly for the most part (Grand Trine with Jupiter and Venus) but with the possibility of explosive endings, with unhappy results (Opposition to Pluto). The Grand Trine in Air reveals a somewhat superficial, but new, intellectual attack on human problems. Notice that the opposition to Pluto almost completes a Grand Trine kite but Venus is just too widely placed. The Sun in Pisces – Moon in Sagittarius polarity shows an excitable, irritable, and over-active personality whereas the Sun in the 1st House – Moon in the 10th House polarity suggests an inner frustration in which an inclination to follow a line of least resistance clashes with an awareness that he needed to assert himself to exploit his creativity. The Sun opposition to Uranus indicates a disruptive personality who, despite his outgoing nature, could easily have been intimidated by competitors. The Moon square Venus suggests an uneasy expression of affections and some difficulty balancing his own needs against those of others. The 1st decanate of Pisces containing the Morin Point shows the presence of an impelling force behind him pushing him unconsciously towards good or ill. Neptune (ruler) in Aquarius in the 12th House indicates his liability to take up vague ideas that tended to increase his rebellious independence.

His Splay-shaped Birth chart (see Figure 16), with its East emphasis indicates an unusual temperament with possible idealistic tendencies that is in charge of its own destiny. The Sun in Sagittarius – Moon in Virgo polarity shows discrimination, power of language and a love of harmony whereas the Sun in the 2nd House – Moon in the 10th House polarity suggests that he coped smoothly and adequately but tended to

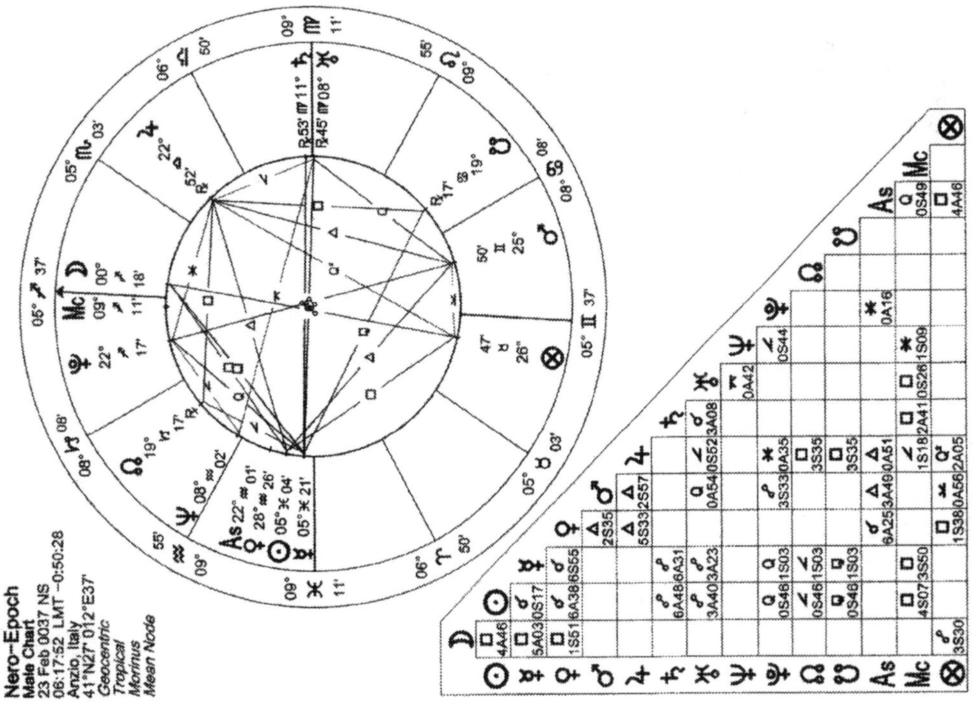

Figure 16: Birth Chart and Aspect Grid for Nero

Nero–Birth
Male Chart
15 Dec 0037 NS
04:34:56 LMT −0:50:28
Anzio, Italy
41°N27′ 012°E37′
Geocentric
Tropical
Morinus
Mean Node

Figure 15: Epoch Chart and Aspect Grid for Nero

Nero–Epoch
Male Chart
23 Feb 0037 NS
06:17:52 LMT −0:50:28
Anzio, Italy
41°N27′ 012°E37′
Geocentric
Tropical
Morinus
Mean Node

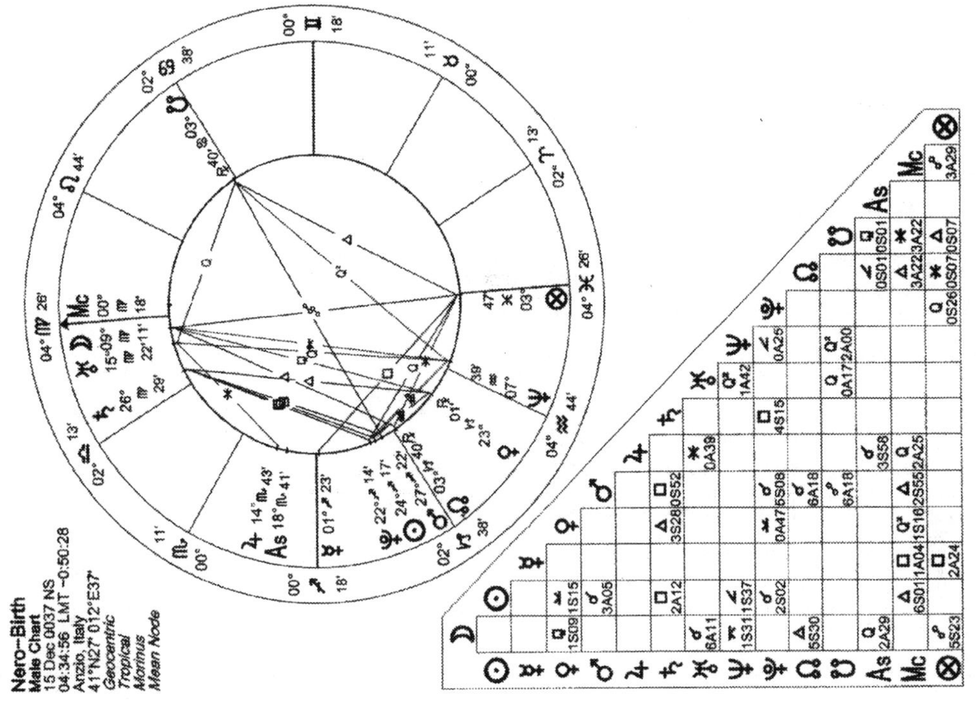

be apathetic. Notice that the Moon in both charts lies in the 10th House strongly indicating a life brought before the public.

The Sun conjoint both Mars and Pluto shows energetic expression, a capacity for hard work and an ability to dispense with the old and begin the new. The square of this triple conjunction to Saturn indicates a hard life that could well lead to self-pity. The Moon sesquiquadrate to Venus confirms his uneasy expression of affection. The Morin Point in the 1st Sagittarius decanate reveals his open-minded, generous disposition but also his uncertain fate. Jupiter (ruler) in Scorpio in the 12th House shows his intense desire for life but accompanied by the risk of pushing himself towards violent behaviour. Mercury rising emphasises his talkativeness. Venus retrograde in Capricorn in the 3rd House shows that he needed to bring something to what he felt was a necessary completion and that he tended to be out of synchronisation in most of his relationships. He was the sort of individual who could easily have felt alone in a crowd. Notice the absence of any substantial Scorpio influence among the three main indicators of his Epoch and Birth charts that could have strengthened his resolve to resist subversives and so remain as emperor.

Person Summary with Biographical Extracts

Character

General: Nero displayed a contrasting set of personality traits. An active, quick, busy-body person, Nero could be irritable, disruptive and awkward. Bold, forceful, noble and initiatory he was rather conceited, vain of his abilities and eager to display his talents. He also tended to be negative, peaceful, methodical and honest showing hospitality and kindness to animals. He was objective, impressionable and fond of liberty, so much so that he was liable to become isolated.

Mentality: Nero's mentality seemed like a mixture of sense and nonsense. His excitable, over-active nature made him talkative, passionate and inspirational but he would also indulge in tittle-tattle and scandal-mongering. At times shallow-minded, he was liable to take up vague ideas that increased his rebellious independence making him seem self-willed and revolutionary. In addition, he was secretive, receptive, scheming and superficial, lacking fixity or mental grasp, but could also be inspired with firm ideas. However, his mentality was keen to work towards a distant ideal. He was sharp and intelligent in small matters showing an open-minded, honest, sympathetic disposition with a teasingly caustic sense of humour. His discrimination, use of language and love of harmony showed balance rather than worry, and charm of speech with ease of writing rather than strength. He could show bright, clear but critical thought and leant towards philosophy, law and order. He was more intuitive than imitative. His approach to initiate a better basis for human society was diverse but tended to lack determination, although he could see opportunities for development in all circumstances of his life. His idealistic, spiritual mind and romantic outlook showed clarity and some religious sentiment. He had the ability to foresee with material things. He also tended to spend much time analysing all that he felt.

Lifestyle: Nero's self-expression was shown energetically in lively enjoyment of love-making, children, games and all pleasures. He also desired widespread activity of mind. He broadened his experience by pleasantness of manner as well as by a strong and intense desire for life. He coupled this with a full appreciation of ease, comfort, luxury, elegance and refinement. His deep feelings and wide sympathies were expressed harmlessly but there was the risk that he pushed himself towards violent behaviour. He could often be reckless, extravagant and careless. His well-intentioned, inner nature tended to fritter its energies in mere dissipation. His inclination to follow the line of least resistance was frustrated by his conscious awareness that he had to assert himself

155

and suffered from varying moods being receptive to the mental atmosphere around him. He often found himself torn between two different emotions thereby hurtfully limiting his self-expression. Yet he didn't neglect to consider how important he was to himself. He had no desire to conserve himself, or his resources, but dug deeply into life and poured forth the results of his gathered experiences with unremitting zeal. Thus his temperament tended to jut out into experience according to its own very special tastes, robustly resisting pigeon-holing. Shotter (see ref.) describes him as follows:

'In present times Nero is the unfulfilled young man with "acute behavioural problems", who wants, constantly, to occupy the centre of attention. Nero was a man of contrasts. "How could he sink to the depths of murdering his mother and his wife?" But look again and we find a man of clemency and generosity that wanted to provide for his people. For example, "Saturnalia" gave him an opportunity to level himself with the interests of his ordinary subjects. All this cannot be explained away by madness. Present representations of Nero fail if they lean too far in this direction, especially when we consider the sound, innovative building principles contained in his architectural projects. His reactions to both his good and bad deeds, although totally self-centred, were thoroughly intelligible.'

The previous, combined, character description basically agrees with Shotter's assessment.

Relationships

<u>Others:</u> Basically Nero was courteous and helpful but his outgoing nature concealed the fact that he was rather easily intimidated by competitors. He kept to himself any doubts about his ability to cope with challenging situations because he would have been ashamed to have had people know about his weaknesses. He felt out-of-tune and insecure with people at or near his own age. For acceptance he would say things that he knew were not true from his point of view but which

would gain the social acceptance that he craved. He judged people by their physical assets, paying little attention to their human qualities.

<u>Acquaintances:</u> Nero cultivated friendships with people who were in a position to help him to achieve the security he wanted. He enjoyed good times with sincere friends in comfortable circumstances and he would always be blessed with these conditions. He hated to turn friends down when they asked him for help.

<u>Family:</u> Nero had a love of home life **but there was uneasy expression of affection and lack of harmony in the home.** He worked diligently for those he loved, especially his children, to give them every advantage that he didn't have. As they succeeded in their way, he would have felt grateful for having had the opportunity to support them.

<u>Partner:</u>   Warmth and enthusiasm entered into Nero's affectionate relationships both in sexual life and as expressed to young people in a family. He was fond of, and improvident with, low company of the opposite sex (as well as of his own, e.g. with Tigillanus). Generally he was out of synchronisation in most of his relationships. Either he loved too much, or too little, compared to the love he received from his partner, or his love was out of tune in the time dimension. Thus he experienced great problems trying to live in the here and now with others. He tended not always to mean what he said but was more interested in the feeling it aroused in the listener. Nero was the kind of individual who could easily feel alone in a crowd. This was a poor situation for marriage. He should have deliberated long and hard before committing himself to a permanent, marital relationship. He had to be sensitive to any residual resentment he retained from his early years that would have disturbed the harmony of his permanent relationship. However, limitation of affection had its reward in a serious, single-minded direction (e.g. with Acte or with Poppaea?) Love may have meant sacrifice or a life lonely except for the chosen one. Partnerships were a serious matter but successful in a practical

duty and to career security could have caused him to neglect his partner leading to resentment.

Career

Early: Maternal conditioning led Nero to believe that he was not qualified to make his own way in life. In fact, he didn't really need to have to prove himself to his mother's satisfaction, only to his own. He had to acquire the appropriate skills to establish his authority in his field as an absolute must for his own sense of worth.   Gaining recognition for his achievements was essential so he used his creative gifts to that end. His enthusiasm allowed him to persist in reaching his goals.   He should have been able to convince his superiors of his qualifications and probably he was offered opportunities to show his abilities. He tended to deny himself pleasure or happiness when young in the hope of some greater promise later. Then he started to make his outlook more practical in terms of his own needs. As a result he seemed mature for his age when young but inside he was rebelling against all the restrictions on his freedom.

He knew that his future was in his own hands. His fate seemed divided between the extremes of fortune and misfortune. External forces constantly created conditions that either he was not yet ready for, or that had already passed him by. His basic survival instincts and the base formed from experiences from his early development were at odds with his desire to achieve in life. As a result he developed difficulties dealing with authority and mistakenly tended to assume that it was determined to obstruct him.

Nero was preoccupied with gaining freedom from want, which was precious to him. Security was his most important consideration and he put a lot of energy into acquiring the necessities of life, to have an advantage over those who lacked them. He needed to fulfil the sense of security he was trying to establish.

He had the ability for public speaking and because he was "tuned" to others' needs, he had the talent and disposition to help others find a more abundant life. He had to serve others before he could serve himself. It may have been difficult but he must not have lost his own identity through helping others. But he also had to realise that others' needs had a high priority and that his personal desires had to come second.

He was a busy and hard worker who could have accomplished much. Success was indicated in affairs of the sea, in businesses to do with oil, painting, music, poetry, dancing, acting, psychism and in hidden and philanthropic work. Shotter comments:

'Whether it was conciliating the senate, reaching good decisions when sitting in judgement, giving rulings that pleased the lower class, attacking corrupt provincial governors, performing in public, organising relief work after the Fire, or planning and building his "People's Palace" his motive, albeit utterly self-indulgent, was always the winning of gratitude and popularity. Like a spoiled child (Epictetus describes Nero as a spoiled, angry and unhappy man), when he succeeded in this aim, his response would be characteristically warm-hearted, as he showed in his "Liberation of Hellos" (he built Greek style gymnasia and theatres showing his 'Philhellenism') but when he did not succeed, then his reaction would consist of tantrums and lashing out, often with great cruelty, against those, who in his view, had let him down.'

Middle: Nero felt an obligation to develop his ideas in any way that would help him to achieve his goals. He needed to bring something to what he felt was a necessary completeness. Some impelling force behind him seemed to push him onward for good or ill, unconsciously. There was a particular and uncompromising direction to his life-effort during which he adapted his allegiances to lines along which he could make his efforts count for the most. His ideas attracted attention and gave him what he needed to realise his goals. His compassionate nature had allowed him to focus sharply on all facets of a problem and on its probable solution. He had been ready to get rid of the old and begin the new. He had met the burdens of old age in his youth and wanted the freedom of his teenage years later. When older he hoped to make up for all that he had missed. Thus his rise to success had followed severe limitations early in life but his enthusiasm had allowed him to persist in reaching his goals. As a result he had derived many benefits from his ability to cope with frustration and he was reasonably aware of what would be expected of him as he rose in his career. His success was then all the more precious to him. He had become suitable for a public career with the ability to elicit the best response from superiors, colleagues and the public. Serving others was fine so long as he did not sacrifice his own personal needs. He became successful and smooth, coping adequately but his hard life, causing him self-pity, had made him apathetic. Shotter concludes:

'The accession of power to Nero highlighted the fatal flaw of a dynastic succession system. He was not the right man for the job but he did possess talent. However, he was too immature so that he was too reliant on others (e.g. Seneca and Burrus) in a way that he resented. Nero was content in his job so long as he could exercise its powers and privileges to win popularity. Alongside his other artistic interests (music, poetry and acting) Nero had a passion for architecture. His buildings portrayed him as a public benefactor, who gladly shared his subjects' enthusiasm.

After the Fire Nero opened his palaces to provide shelter for the homeless and arranged for food supplies to prevent starvation. The ensuing reconstruction of Rome followed sound building principles allowing for a decent life-style in a ground-breaking, architectural style (he also filled the marshes of Ostia with the rubble from the Fire).'

<u>Late:</u> He had wanted to be independent so that he could enjoy his later years without being obligated to anyone. He had been fortunate materially so that he was no longer too preoccupied with future security because he had made the necessary plans to solve that problem.

Health

General: Although physically robust, he suffered from neuralgia springing from over-repression in his unconscious life. There was also trouble through subversive effects of intuition and psychic power or in hidden and mediumistic ways. Additionally, he had a tendency to falls, (he nearly died from a chariot accident while in Greece) chills and orthopaedic troubles.

Appearance: Overall Nero was of medium stature, handsome with a rounded visage, possibly large nose, sanguine but fair complexion and light brown hair. ("about the average height, his body marked with spots and malodorous, his hair light blond, regular features rather than attractive, blue, somewhat weak eyes, over-thick neck, prominent belly and very slender legs" – Suetonius).

Activities: He was fond of games and sports. He liked the water and probably was a good swimmer, like his mother. 'Nero sang to the harp (firstly in private and then at the second Neronia), composed songs and wrote poetry.'

Reference: "Nero; Caesar Augustus", David Shotter, Pearson Education Ltd., Harlow, Middlesex, U.K., 2008.

- -

DOMITIAN

"The sombre but intelligent despotism of Domitian" – T Mommsen

As emperor, in a reign that lasted 15 years (81 – 96 A.D.), Domitian strengthened the economy by revaluing the Roman coinage, expanded the border defences of his empire and initiated a massive building programme to restore the fire-damaged city of Rome, particularly the library. He received the education of a young man of the privileged senatorial class. He was described as a learned and educated adolescent. He was tall of stature, with a modest expression and a high colour. His eyes were large but his sight was somewhat dim. By way of contradiction, he showed considerable marksmanship with the bow and arrow. He was handsome and graceful when a young man except for his toes that were cramped. He became bald early, developed a protruding belly and spindly legs following a long illness. He appears to have lacked the charisma of his elder brother, Titus, and of his father, Vespasian. He was prone to suspicion, displayed self-deprecating humour and communicated cryptically. As he became older he became more solitary; that may have stemmed from his isolated upbringing. He had a long marriage and one son, who died young. He saw himself as a new Augustus, an enlightened despot destined to guide the Roman Empire into a new era. As a result Domitian was popular with the people and the army but despised by members of the Senate (a small but highly-vocal minority who exaggerated his despotism) as a tyrant. There was no widespread dissatisfaction with him; his hardness was reserved for the Senate. His foreign policy was realistic; rejecting expansion and negotiating peace at a time when Rome traditionally dictated aggressive conquest.   However, significant wars were fought in Britain and in Dacia but he was unable to subdue Decebalus properly.   Persecution of religious minorities was non-existent.   By nominating himself as perpetual censor he sought to control public and private morals.   He restricted freedom of speech and adopted an increasingly oppressive attitude towards the Senate. He became involved with all branches of government and successfully prosecuted corruption among public officials.   In his later reign, executions, deriving from his suspicious nature, became known as "the terror".   Eventually he was assassinated by court officials.   During his reign the Roman Empire prospered between 81 and 96 A.D.   Modern history characterises him as a ruthless but efficient autocrat whose cultural, economic and political programme provided the foundation of the peaceful 2nd century.

Domitian - Horoscopes

Domitian was born on the 24th October, 51 A.D., at 20:13, in Rome, Italy, the 2nd son of Vespasian and Domitilla. His Epoch* occurred on the 6th February, 51 A.D., at 01:36. His Epoch chart (see Figure 17) shows that the planets lie mainly in the North East quadrant suggesting a mixture of self-determination and subjectivity.   The chart shaping is a bundle type bucket with the Moon as a West single -ton, which suggests, overall, a rather narrow yet particular direction

- -

*At birth the Moon was above the Earth and increasing in light making his Epoch 1st Order. His Morin Point occupied a female area and the Moon a male one. The Regular Sex Epoch seems the most likely rather than either of the other possible Irregular Sex Epochs of the 2nd and 3rd Variation for a male birth.

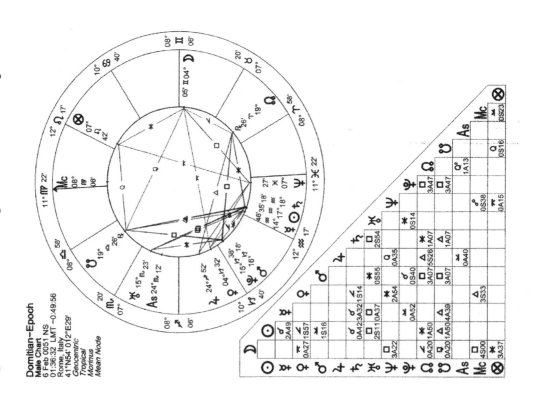

Figure 18: Domitian's Birth Chart and Aspect Grid

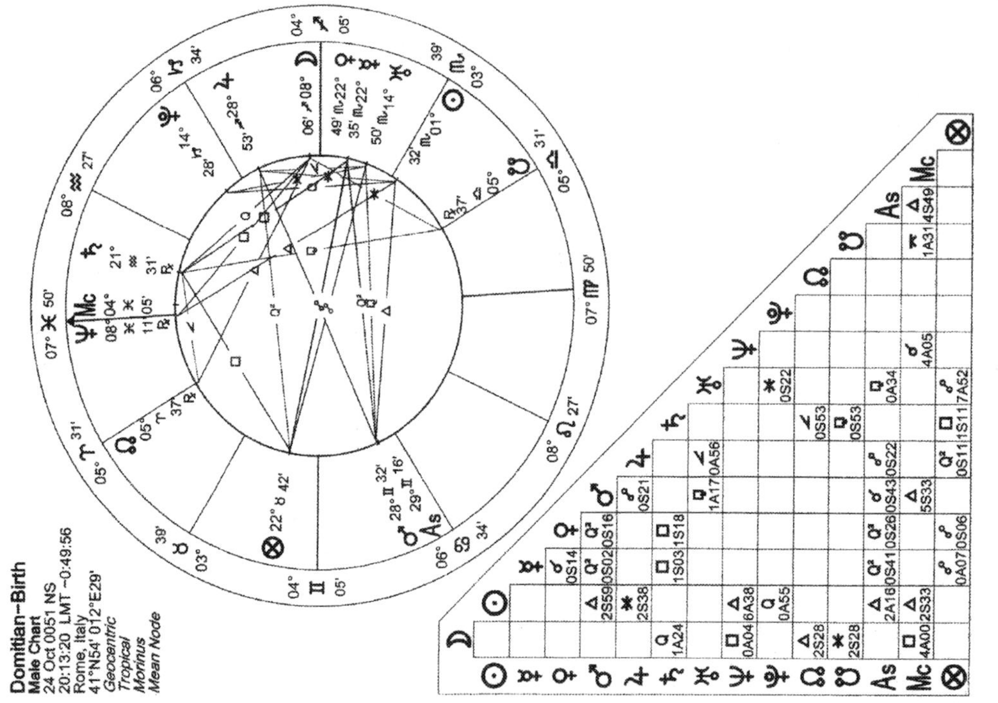

Figure 17: Domitian's Epoch Chart and Aspect Grid

164

to his life-effort. The Moon in the 7th House indicates that stability could have been supplied by a permanent partner. The Sun in Aquarius – Moon in Gemini polarity shows intellectual qualities coupled with a neat, well-stored mind. The Sun in the 3rd House – Moon in the 7th House reveals a deep, but apprehensive, need to relate to others. The Sun conjoint Saturn suggests that he felt inadequate when dealing with the common people, neighbours and siblings. Whereas the Sun/Mercury conjunction square Uranus implies communication that is too brusque, it also shows an ideas person. **The Moon square to Neptune** reveals tendencies to escapism, deceit and self-gullibility. His Morin Point in the 1st Sagittarius decanate suggests openness, independence, impressionability and someone who could also be priggish. The ruler, Jupiter, in Sagittarius in the 2nd House, denotes fineness of character with dignity but without pomposity. His Epoch generates his Ideal Birth chart (see Figure 18). This chart shows that the planets lie mainly to the West indicating that prevailing circumstances would influence his life direction. As with his Epoch chart, we see a bundle type bucket shaping with Mars as the East singleton planet in Gemini in the 2nd House. Energetically talkative, he would have had a strong interest in financial and agricultural matters. There is almost a Grand-Trine kite about the Mars/Jupiter opposition – only Neptune is placed just too widely. This increases the focus on Mars but eases the difficulty of its opposition to Jupiter with the sextile/trine combination with the Sun. This suggests that his versatility and opportunism could provide some helpful diversion to his wild extravagance of thought and deed. The Sun in Scorpio – Moon in Sagittarius polarity shows combativeness and rash action but also conservatism combined with progressive ideas. The Sun in the 6th House – Moon in the 7th House polarity again suggests that he was ineffective in social situations and also that his suspicious nature probably derived from the treatment he received from people. The Sun trine Mars and sextile to Jupiter implies a bold, yet acceptable disposition and good luck coupled with good opportunities. As with his Epoch, **the Moon square Neptune** suggests great sensitivity but also deceit and self-deception. The Morin Point in the 1st Gemini decanate reveals his kind, intellectual and expressive disposition and the ruler, Mercury, in Scorpio, closely conjoint Venus, shows mental intensity and penetration but that these are softened to give balance rather than worry. The biquintile of Mercury to Mars provides forcefulness and incisiveness, whereas the square to Saturn, although constructive in a narrow way, could also produce rigid discipline and dreary planning.

Notice that Domitian had one major indicator (the Sun at birth) in the 1st Scorpio decanate that could have accounted for his ruthlessness.

Domitian – Person Summary with Biographical Extracts

Character

General: Domitian's fine character showed dignity without pomposity. He was kind, willing, good-hearted, humane, sympathetic, generous and philanthropic.

Mentality: As a humanitarian (Domitian administered justice scrupulously and conscientiously; he consistently treated aristocrats and others in the same fashion) he showed an interest in science (Astrology) and detachment. 'He lacked hypocrisy, persecuting neither Christians nor Jews. He risked obloquy through his utter determination to govern according to his own standards, to ignore tradition when it did not suit him and to proclaim the Senate's impotence rather than disguise it through platitudes. He emphasised the development of a power set. Basically, he was a monarch. Probably he was the only emperor who could have decided to withdraw from Britain completely.' He had an innate conservatism combined with progressive ideas. His enterprising, open, impressionable, studious and well-stored mind (Domitian had received a good education and was trained in rhetoric. His speech to the Senate, aged 18, was brief, restrained and well-defended. He wrote poetry in his twenties, could quote from Homer and Vergil and had published a book on baldness), coupled with a good memory, gave him the intellectual and expressive disposition that enabled his oratorical power. Although his curiosity, desire to learn about many subjects and his clever/inventive abilities were held in check, his concentration and discrimination were enhanced (he loved everything Greek, publically he associated Jupiter with his regime but privately his devotion to Minerva was absolute - he began to rebuild the library at Alexandria). Neatness, industry and perfection with regard to details came naturally to him. He was mentally intense and penetrative but his mental outlook was softened, showing balance rather than worry.

Energetically talkative, lively, forceful, incisive, and insistent Domitian was full of ideas and good at debate. However, combativeness with tendencies to sarcasm followed by indiscreet and explosive speech and writing, strong impulse and rash action, revealed the wild extravagance of thought and deed beneath. Then there was danger of extremism in both work and play. 'As a young man he had indulged in debauchery and adultery.' The resulting lack of poise forced a brusque and independent attitude that lost good contact with others ("the better one knew him, the less one could like him"). The fear and apprehension of the resulting mental loneliness could have led to rigid discipline and boredom when planning (Domitian's administration may not have liked him but they would have obeyed him). He had great sensitivity but seemed to be open to gullibility (he also became suspicious).

<u>Lifestyle:</u> Generally, Domitian's bold self-expression, fondness for liberty and independence failed to annoy others. He was cheerful and contented with his own surroundings, loved law and order but probably was over-shrewd and hard. He was susceptible to subversive influences (he employed informers; the Emperor's character declined from clemency to suspicion; treasonable "cowardly" foreign policy remarks became punishable) with a tendency to escapism (he preferred to live and act away from Rome and the Senate) but refrained from starting rumours himself. Occasionally his explosive, terrible anger almost certainly ended conditions and so forced new beginnings.

Relationships

<u>Others:</u> Domitian's social contacts and alliances were held in check. 'Domitian lived a solitary life behind closed doors and went for solitary walks after a meal. Drinking competitions stopped and he showed an interest in brain and literary contests at the Games. He seemed to be "socially incompetent".' His feelings were inadequate when dealing with common people, neighbours and even siblings. 'He showed no brotherly affection to Titus when he was dying.' Although he had a deep need to relate to others professionally and socially, his early family ties had made him inwardly apprehensive that he would be rejected. 'He had had to wait years for "imperium" and for genuine responsibility.' While not particularly effective socially, he was versatile and opportunistic. He willingly listened to the ideas of others, thereby enriching them, but he tended to give people the benefit of the doubt, which meant that he may have indulged them unnecessarily. He should have been wary of people who always turned to him for help with their problems because often, they would have taken advantage of him.

<u>Friends:</u> Domitian made many acquaintances if few friends. He preferred women as close friends. He was wary about forming close ties with associates or with people who showed a romantic interest in him. He studied these contacts carefully to learn people's motivations for wanting to become aligned with him.

<u>Family:</u> Domitian's parents probably provided him with reasonable training.

<u>Lover/Partner:</u> Domitian's ability to love and enjoy sexual life and all things of beauty was strong and robust but not delicate. He was changeful towards those in any close relationship probably because he found affection difficult to express. His depth of feeling in affairs to do with partnership, or in any matter requiring rapport or reciprocity with others, was expressed in hurtful ways (uncertainty soon gave way to fear). Possibly a disappointing childhood conditioned him to escape into marriage with a partner who would have been motherly. 'He married Domitia Longina (a daughter of Corbulo, a motherly-looking woman) and maintained a genuine affection for her throughout their long marriage.'

Career

<u>Early:</u> Domitian's early circumstances allowed him to express himself and become involved in the world around him. Additionally his education helped him to face life's hazards more objectively. His life advanced through his educational and intellectual attainments. His destiny lay in his own hands (he knew what he wanted) as well as in prevailing conditions. Good luck was to be expected along with plenty of opportunities. However, his life was held within several narrow bands of opportunism (Domitian was eager for military glory but was never given the chance for it), tending to inhibit him, with the exception, in his case, that a permanent partner gave him emotional comfort so that he could direct his efforts

towards his career. In return, he derived much satisfaction from indulging his mate. His life was rigorous but lessons of duty and self-control were well-learnt. 'When still a teenager he became a figurehead emperor while his father and elder brother were on campaign against the Jews, but in reality Mucianus was the power at the helm behind the scenes.' There was a particular and uncompromising direction to his life-effort. He was a busy, enthusiastic and practical worker for any cause that he espoused. 'His ideal for an emperor included a specific, cultural role as well as a political one that were to be the source of encouragement for the future and for his own glory.' He was a good soldier and/or religious, legal or medical leader (he appointed himself as the empire's perpetual censor). Additionally, he would have excelled in a career in education, counselling, selling, politics, and social service or with children with learning difficulties, who require sympathetic understanding. He would have been able to show them how to become self-sufficient (reportedly and unfortunately he enjoyed sex with boys). Above all perhaps, he was a pioneer in financial and agricultural matters (of major concern to him was the supply of corn to Rome and to the rest of the empire).

Middle: Domitian was constructive in a narrow way. However, forcefully pragmatic, he satisfied his urge for creative expression by using his effective communication skills. He had a talent for making the most of these basic skills and his resources. He had little concern over end-results and no basic desire for self-preservation or for conserving his resources. He adapted his allegiances to lines along which he could make his efforts count for the most. He dipped deeply into life and poured forth his gathered experiences with unremitting zeal. At his best he was an instructor and inspirer of others. Working with the public and offering services that were in constant demand gave him reassuring feedback about his own competence. He could win recognition for his ability to deal with the public provided he was sincerely concerned to help them solve their problems (he treated malefactors equally, irrespective of their public standing). In the back of his mind there was a desire to help others build their own future. To this end he used his own life as a model to show others how to adapt their skills to take advantage of opportunity.

Domitian expected to be paid well for good work. He needed a lot of money because he spent freely. 'The economy was his special concern. To emulate Augustus he laid out a massive building program to rebuild Rome, especially the library, after the Fire. He had to revise his early generosity and to balance his budget (Domitian inherited and bequeathed a balanced budget) he resorted to confiscations and rigorous tax collection.' He enjoyed having money and got much satisfaction from knowing that his creative abilities were appreciated and he didn't want to be obligated to others. When he observed others achieving financial security from their endeavours he was stimulated to match or surpass their performance. He found it exciting to have the opportunity of handling other people's assets and indeed, financial counselling would have provided an attractive career for him.

Late: Domitian came to over-estimate his power to the extent that people resented it. 'He was assassinated by his own courtiers. He had executed two of them. For him, this was the beginning of the end. For them, his inability to work with them had been the last straw.'

Health

Domitian had a strong nervous system resulting in good eyesight (he was a talented archer), hearing and sense of smell (he loved hunting) but he still tended to over-strain through "overdoing it".

Appearance: Domitian had a somewhat long face, nose, chin, arms and fingers. He was tall, erect, inclined to baldness and walked keenly with speed. He was physically muscular with a powerful voice that may have been discordant.

Reference: "The Emperor Domitian", Brian W Jones, Routledge, London, 1993.

- -

APPENDIX 4

Epoch and Birth Charts of the Rest of the 2ⁿᵈ Tier Power Notables

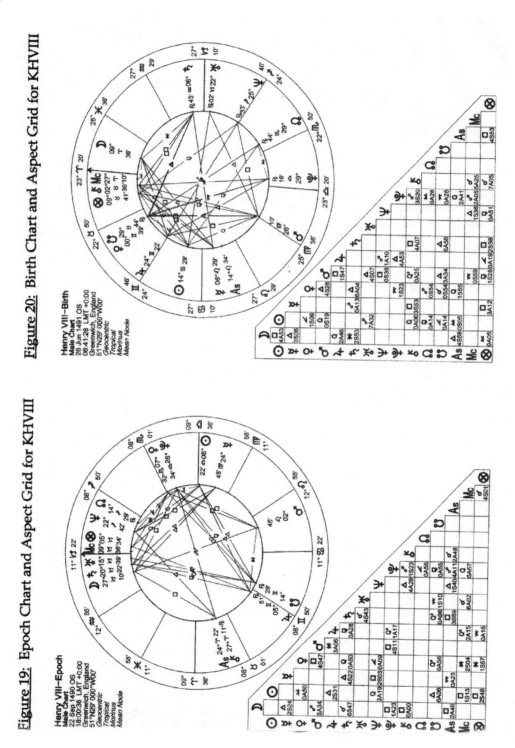

Figure 20: Birth Chart and Aspect Grid for KHVIII

Figure 19: Epoch Chart and Aspect Grid for KHVIII

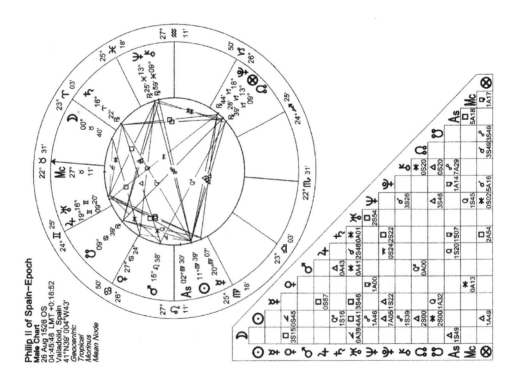

Figure 21: King Philip II Epoch Chart and Aspect Grid

Figure 22: King Philip II Birth Chart and Aspect Grid

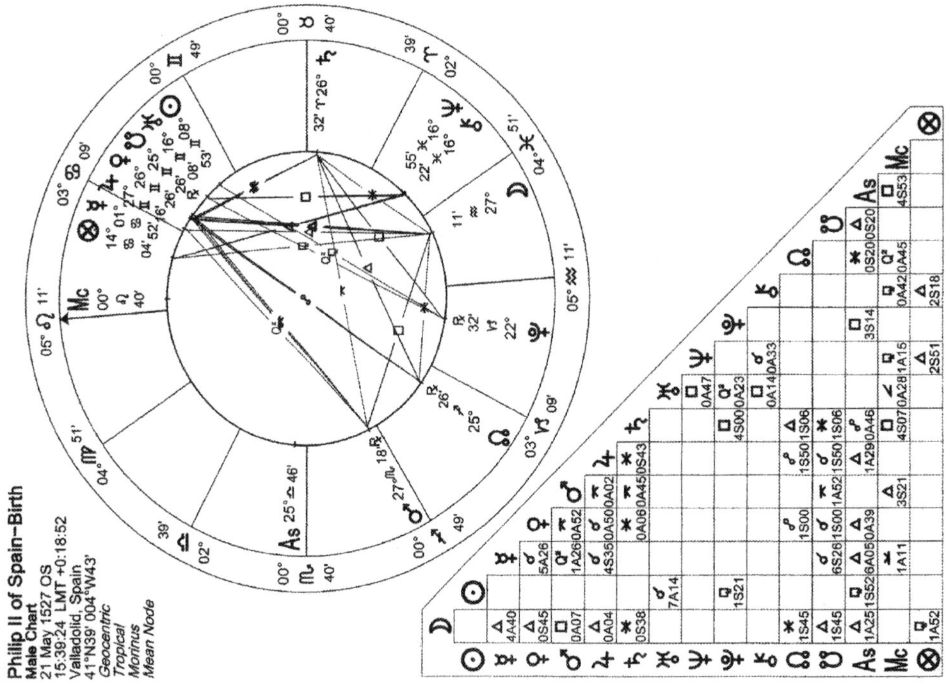

Figure 24: Elizabeth I's Birth Chart and Aspect Grid

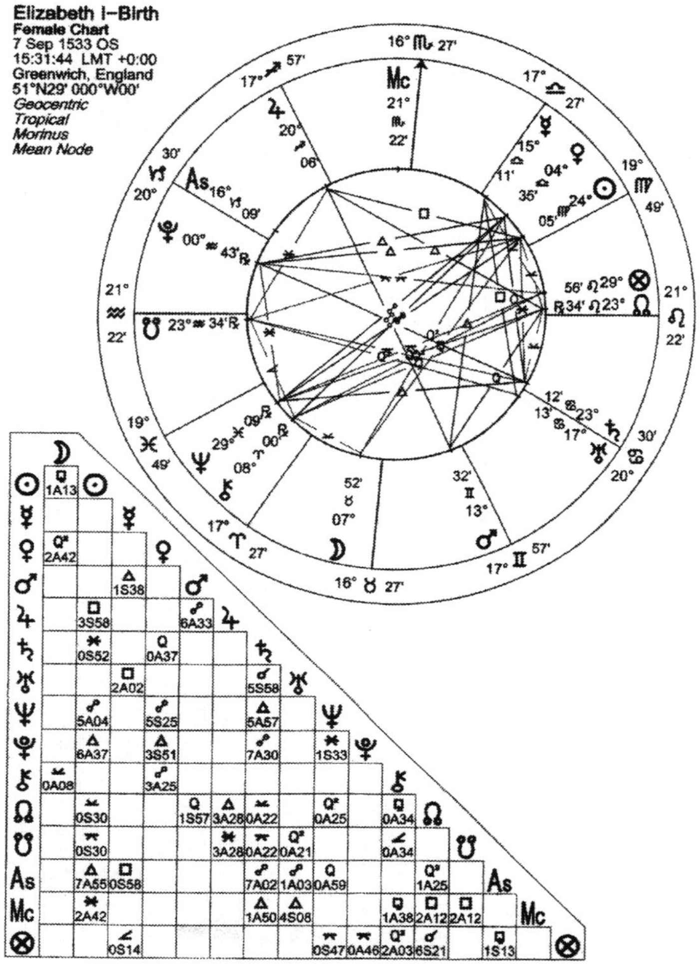

Figure 23: Elizabeth I's Epoch Chart and Aspect Grid

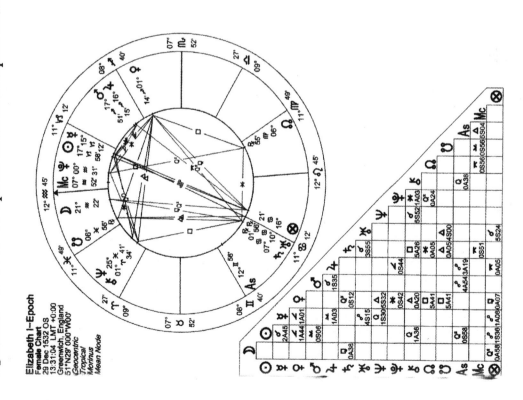

175

Figure 25: Epoch Chart and Aspect Grid for O. Cromwell   Figure 26: Birth Chart and Aspect Grid for O. Cromwell

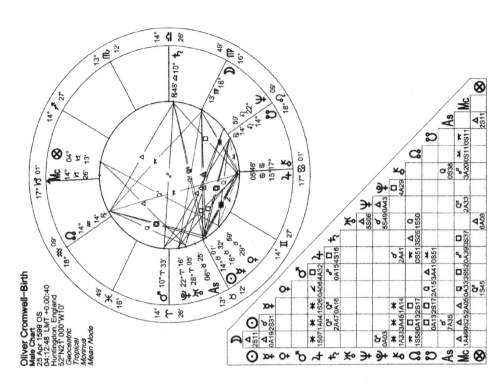

Oliver Cromwell–Birth
Male Chart
25 Apr 1599 OS
04:12:48 LMT +0:00:40
Huntingdon, England
52°N21' 000°W10'
Geocentric
Tropical
Morinus
Mean Node

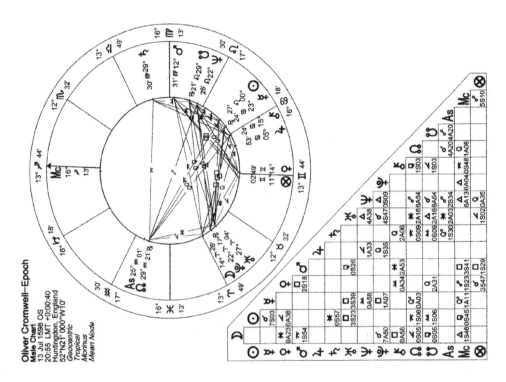

Oliver Cromwell–Epoch
Male Chart
13 Jul 1598 OS
20:55 LMT +0:00:40
Huntingdon, England
52°N21' 000°W10'
Geocentric
Tropical
Morinus
Mean Node

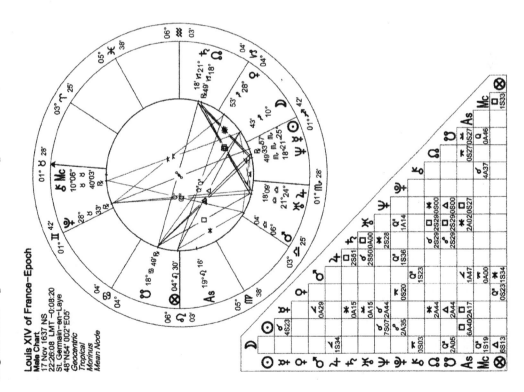

Figure 27: Epoch Chart and Aspect Grid for Louis XIV

Figure 28: Birth Chart and Aspect Grid for Louis XIV

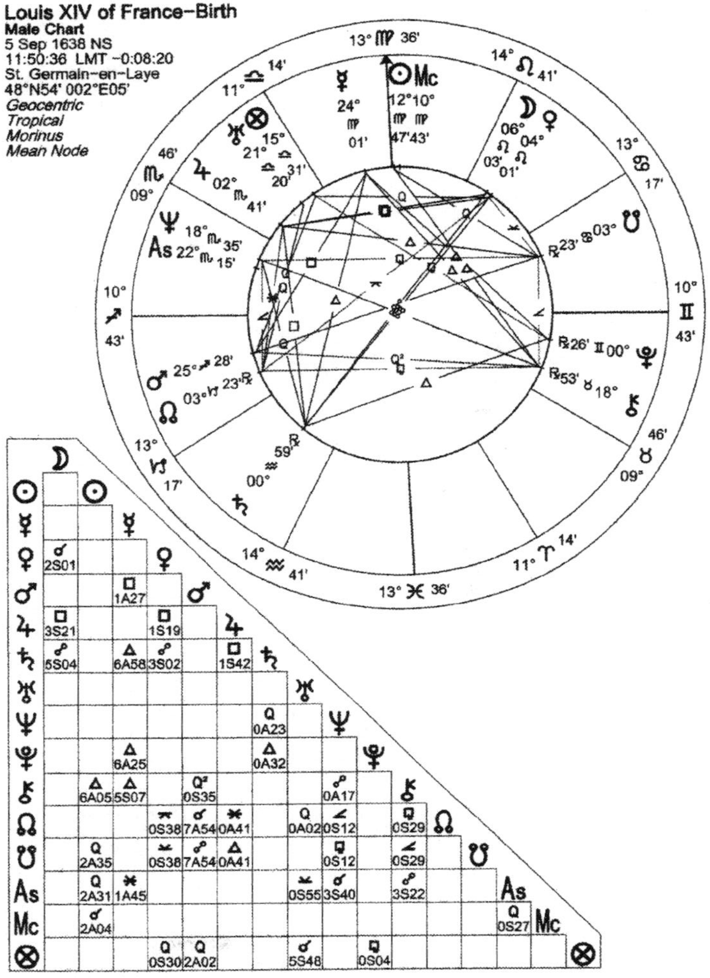

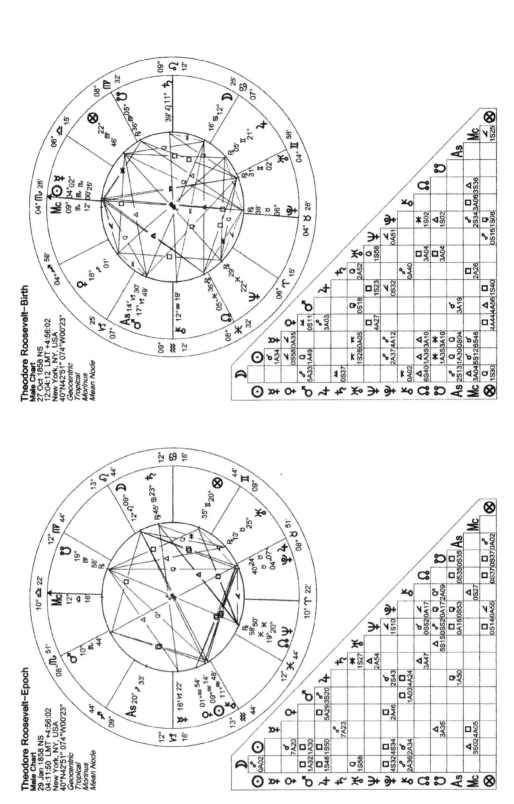

Figure 29: Epoch Chart and Aspect Grid for T. Roosevelt Figure 30: Birth Chart and Aspect Grid for T. Roosevelt